THE SEVEN AGAINST THEBES

BY AESCHYLUS

PRENTICE-HALL  *GREEK DRAMA SERIES*

Series Editors

ERIC A. HAVELOCK, *Sterling Professor of Classics, Yale University*
MAYNARD MACK, *Sterling Professor of English, Yale University*

	Translated with commentary by
AESCHYLUS	
Agamemnon	Hugh Lloyd-Jones
The Eumenides	Hugh Lloyd-Jones
The Libation Bearers	Hugh Lloyd-Jones
The Persians	Anthony J. Podlecki
Prometheus Bound	Eric A. Havelock
The Seven Against Thebes	Christopher M. Dawson
SOPHOCLES	
Ajax	Adam M. Parry
Antigone	Anne Amory
Electra	William Sale
Oedipus at Colonus	Joseph A. Russo
Oedipus the King	Thomas Gould
Philoctetes	William Arrowsmith
The Women of Trachis	Peter W. Rose
EURIPIDES	
Alcestis	Charles Rowan Beye
The Bacchae	Geoffrey S. Kirk
Electra	Wesley Smith
Heracles	Christian Wolff
Hippolytus	Gilbert & Sally Lawall
Ion	Anne Pippin Burnett
Iphigenia in Aulis	Kenneth Cavander
Medea	Bernard M. W. Knox
The Suppliants	A. Thomas Cole

The remaining nine plays are in preparation.

THE seven against THEBES

BY æSCHYLUS

A Translation with Commentary by

CHRISTOPHER M. DAWSON

Talcott Professor of Greek

Yale University

with a series introduction by Eric A. Havelock

PRENTICE-HALL, INC., ENGLEWOOD CLIFFS, N.J.

C13–806851–8
P13–806844–5

Library of Congress Catalog Card Number: 78–102293
Printed in the United States of America

Current Printing (last number):
10 9 8 7 6 5 4 3 2 1

PRENTICE-HALL INTERNATIONAL, INC. *London*
PRENTICE-HALL OF AUSTRALIA, PTY. LTD. *Sydney*
PRENTICE-HALL OF CANADA, LTD. *Toronto*
PRENTICE-HALL OF INDIA PRIVATE LIMITED *New Delhi*
PRENTICE-HALL OF JAPAN, INC. *Tokyo*

In Memory of
Marjorie

CONTENTS

CONTENTS

FOREWORD TO THE SERIES

The Prentice-Hall Greek Drama Series will contain when completed the surviving tragedies of the Athenian stage. It offers each play in a separate inexpensive volume, so that readers may make their own personal selection rather than have the choice made for them, as is commonly the result when translations are issued in collective groups. It also offers each play in a context of exacting scholarship which seeks to make available to Greekless readers what the original Greek audiences responded to as they watched and listened to a performance. Under the English dress, in short, as far as humanly possible the Greek identity has been accentuated rather than obscured. Supported here by extensive introductions, notes, and appendices (in each case the work of an authority who has given painstaking attention to the full meanings of the text) and printed in a manner to exhibit their great varieties of formal structure, they step forth, untrammeled by preconceptions and conventional categorizations, as the highly individual creations they were when first performed.

The notes printed at the foot of each page to accompany the appropriate lines are in the first instance conceived as a corrective to shortcomings that no translation can avoid and should therefore be considered as in some sense an extension of the text. They testify to the fact that all translations in varying degree must indulge an element of deception, and they serve as a running attempt to explain its character and define its extent. In addition to this, they undertake to instruct the reader about conventions of idiom and imagery, of legend and allusion, which are native to the Greek situation and indispensable to a proper understanding of it. They aim also to get to the heart of the play as a work of art, exposing and explicating its often complex design in the hope that the reader thus aided will experience for himself its overwhelming dramatic effect.

M. M.

THE ATHENIAN DRAMATISTS

(Dates attested or probable are italicized)

AESCHYLUS 525–456		SOPHOCLES 497/6–405/4		EURIPIDES 485/4–406/5	
Total production:	c.90	Total production:	c.125	Total production:	c.92
Surviving plays:	7	Surviving plays:	7*	Surviving plays:	17*
First success	*485*	First success	469	First success	*441*

AESCHYLUS	SOPHOCLES	EURIPIDES
The Persians 472 *The Seven Against Thebes 467* *The Suppliants* 463?	*Ajax* 460–45? (date unknown—probably the earliest)	
Oresteia 458 (*Agamemnon, The Libation Bearers, The Eumenides*)	*Antigone 442–41*	*Alcestis 438*
Prometheus Bound (date unknown probably late)	*The Women of Trachis* (date unknown)	*Medea 431* *The Children of Heracles* c. 430–20
	Oedipus the King 429–25?	*Hippolytus 428* *Hecuba* c. 425
	Electra 420–10	*The Suppliants* c. 420 *Heracles* c. 420–16? *Andromache* c. 419 *Electra* c. *415–13* *The Trojan Women* 415 *Helen 412* *Iphigeneia in Tauris* c. 412 *The Phoenician Women* 410–9
	Philoctetes 409	*Orestes 408* *Ion* c. 408?
	Oedipus at Colonus c. *406–5* (produced posthumously)	*The Bacchae* c. *406* (produced posthumously) *Iphigeneia at Aulis* *406* (produced posthumously)

* disregarding *The Ichneutae* of Sophocles and *The Cyclops* and *Rhesus* of Euripides which are not tragedies.

INTRODUCTION TO THE SERIES

1. GREEK TRAGEDY TODAY

The table of the three tragedians and their productions facing this page reveals a situation which, judged by our experience of European drama since the Greeks, is, to say the least, unusual. The total of thirty-one plays was composed within a span of about sixty-five years, between 472 and 406 B.C., and that ends the story. It is as though the history of the English drama were confined to the Elizabethans and the Jacobeans and then closed. These thirty-one are survivors—a mere handful—of an originally enormous total. The three playwrights between them are credited with over three hundred titles, and the plays of their competitors, which except for isolated fragments and notices have now vanished from the record, are uncountable.

These facts shed light upon a familiar paradox: Classic Greek drama is at once parochial and universal, narrowly concentrated upon recurrent motifs, characters, and situations, yet always able to evoke a response at a level which is fundamental and general. Most of these hundreds of plays were composed in the years between the defeat of the Persians by the Greeks at Salamis in 480 B.C. and the defeat of Athens by Sparta in 404 B.C.; they were produced for audiences in Athens and in Attica, that small canton district which contains the city and is itself circumscribed by the sea and the mountains. The limits of history and geography surrounding them are therefore narrow and intense. Greek tragedy is Attic and Athenian not accidentally but essentially, and this fact cannot but have had strong influence in the dramatic choices made by the playwrights as they selected situation, theme, and characters. The vast bulk of the lost productions, had it been preserved, would, one suspects, retain interest today mainly for specialists and antiquarians. There is indeed a good deal of antiquarianism in the plays we do have. But they are products of their authors' maturity, none composed at an age earlier than forty-five. Their preservation, if we except a few plays of Euripides, reflects some value judgments passed in antiquity; they were on the whole better able to withstand changes of taste and fashion and shifts in the character and nationality of audiences and critics.

The present age has come to recognize a new-found affinity with them. During the last century and the early part of the present one, when study of the classics was still dominant in education, Greek drama was read and esteemed as an exercise in the grand style, a mirror of the eternal verities and familiar moral imperatives. Even Euripides, the least tractable of the three from the moral standpoint, was credited with a desire to set the world right. By and large, the watchword the Victorians heard in the plays was not danger but decorum. Today, a generation which has known frustration and disillusionment—desperately demanding some private identity within a society which seems imprisoned and perhaps doomed by its own prior commitments—can view these plays with clearer eyes for what they are: portrayals of the human dilemma which forswear the luxury of moral confidence and assured solutions. Here are sufferings disproportionate to the original error, characters caught and trapped in situations which are too much for them and for which they are only partly responsible. Here are pity and terror treated as facts of life with which one must come to terms. Here finally is defiance combined with a fatalism which accepts the tragic scene even at the moment of its repudiation. The watchword we listen to today is not decorum but danger. For the children of men who now inherit the earth it is therefore possible to respond to the classic tragedy of the Greeks with a directness denied to the more secure temper of their forebears.

Translators of Greek drama face a difficult choice between editing the Greek into language which will appeal to the modern sensibility, or offering a version which attempts as close an approximation as possible to the form and content of the original. The present series has been conceived on the assumption that since form and content hang together, the one cannot be paraphrased without damaging the other. The damage usually is done by suppressing those features of the original which affront the modern sensibility, while exaggerating those that do not. Quite commonly the operatic form of the plays is in a modern version played down or even ignored, and the temptation is always strong so to interpret the plots as to center interest upon characters at the expense of situation. The versions offered in this series, while modest in their pretensions, have sought to maintain fidelity to that original convention of the Greek which divided the diction of a play between choric and lyric portions on the one hand and spoken dialogue on the other. The two together constituted the total dramatic statement, which was thus partly sung and partly recited, and they are here printed in different typefaces to bring out more clearly the way in which the play's structure is articulated. Passages in hexameters, anapests, and trochaic tetrameters were either sung or chanted, and accordingly are printed here as lyric. The notes also make some attempt to indicate the metrical arrangements practiced in the lyric portions and the emotional effects produced. To transfer these effects in translation from an inflected tongue quantitatively scanned is impossible, and the aids offered are therefore directed to the imagination of the reader rather than to his ear.

2. THE DRAMATISTS

The alienation of the artist is not a condition which the Greeks of the classical age would readily have understood. The three Greek tragedians were Attic born and men of their time, participating, as the record indicates, in the political and social life of their community. Their plays accordingly expose, examine, and question the values of Greek society, but they do not reformulate and they do not reject. This being said, one must add that differences of style and approach between them are marked. The grandiloquence of Aeschylus becomes an appropriate instrument for expressing the confident ethos of the Athenian democracy and a theology which would justify the ways of Zeus to men. In the more stringent style of Sophocles, the tragic hero and heroine endure an exposure which is often ironic but which penetrates to the core of their dilemma, while their essential dignity is preserved and even enhanced. Euripides, the "most tragic" of the three, comes nearest to stepping outside his society. His later plays in particular tend to place the traditional norms of heroic and aristocratic leadership in an equivocal light. But his plots, as they enlarge the roles of women, children, servants, and slaves, remain faithful also to the changing mores and manners which increasingly foreshadowed the individualism of the Hellenistic age.

AESCHYLUS was born c. 525–24 at Eleusis near Athens of an aristocratic family (*eupatrid*). At thirty-five he fought at Marathon, where his brother fell gloriously; he may have also fought at Salamis. He paid two visits to the court of Hieron in Sicily, who was the patron likewise of Pindar, Bacchylides, and Simonides. At the first visit he composed a play for the court celebrating Hieron's founding of the new city of Aetna (after 476); the second visit was terminated by his death at Gela in his seventieth year (456), where an epitaph on his monument celebrated his service at Marathon. An Athenian decree subsequently provided for the revival of any of his plays at public expense. Though he was preceded in the composition of tragic drama by the semi-legendary Thespis, Aeschylus is for practical purposes the "founder" of this unique art form, combining choric performance with a plot supported by dialogue between two, later three, actors. He was both composer and actor-manager, taking leads himself in some of his plays, probably the early ones. He is credited with developing the conventions of grandiloquent diction, rich costuming, formal dance figures, and some degree of spectacular effect. Although he died only about fifty years before *The Frogs* appeared, by Aristophanes' day his life was already a legend. Later stories about him (e.g., that he was an "initiate" who betrayed the secret of the Mysteries, or that he retired to Sicily in discomfiture for a variety of alleged reasons) are probably the inventions of an age more biographically inclined than his own.

SOPHOCLES was born c. 496 of an affluent family at Colonus near Athens. Known for his good looks, he was also an accomplished dancer and lyre player who, at age sixteen, was selected to lead the paean of victory after Salamis. He was taught by Lamprus, a famous master of the traditional music. He played roles in some of his own early productions, but later desisted, because of his weak voice. He took considerable part in public life. In 443–42 he was imperial treasurer; he was elected general twice —once in 440, the year in which Pericles suppressed the revolt of Samos, and again at a later date as colleague of Nicias; also, in 413, when he was over eighty years old, he was appointed one of the special commissioners (*probouloi*) to review the aftermath of the Sicilian disaster. He held a lay priesthood in the cult of a local deity of healing and allowed his own house to serve as a shrine of Asclepius pending the completion of a temple. He founded an Association (*thiasos*) of the Muses (something like a literary club). Polygnotus painted a portrait of him holding the lyre, which was hung in the picture gallery on the Acropolis. Tradition connects him with prominent men of letters, such as Ion of Chios, Herodotus (there are discernible points of contact between the History and the plays), and Archelaus the philosopher. In 406 he mourned the death of his younger contemporary Euripides in a public appearance with actors and chorus at the rehearsal (*proagon*) for the Great Dionysia. Some months later he died, at the age of ninety. He was remembered and celebrated as an example of the fortunate life, genial, accomplished, and serene.

Euripides was born c. 485 at Phlya in Attica, probably of a good family. He made his home in Salamis, probably on an estate of his father, where it is said he composed in a cave by the sea. He held a lay priesthood in the cult of Zeus at his birthplace. Tradition, supported by hints in Old Comedy and the internal evidence of his own plays, connects him with the leading sophistic and philosophical circles of the day: Anaxagoras, Archelaus, Prodicus, Protagoras, and above all Socrates, said to be an admirer of his plays. In musical composition, he was assisted by a certain Cephisophon; this collaboration was probably a common practice. He served on an embassy to Syracuse (date unknown) and composed a public elegy in 413 for the Athenian soldiers fallen in Sicily. Prisoners in the quarries are said to have won release from their captors by reciting his choruses. He appears to have preferred a life of some seclusion, surrounded by his household. In 408–7 he left Athens for the north. He stayed initially at Magnesia in Thessaly, where he was received with honors, and then at the court of Archelaus of Macedon. There, in addition to a court play composed in the king's honor, he produced *The Bacchae*, his last extant work. He died there in 406. Buried in Macedonia he was memorialized by a cenotaph at Athens. Some of his plays were produced posthumously by one of his three sons. A good deal of the tradition surrounding his parentage, domestic life, personal character, and contemporary reputation in Athens is unfriendly to him; but it is also unreliable, depending as it probably does on the satirical treatment which he often received from the comic poets.

3. THE TIMES

In 525, when Aeschylus was born, the "tyranny" established at Athens under Pisistratus and his sons was still in power. When he was fifteen years old, the tyrants were expelled, and a series of constitutional changes began which were to result in the establishment of complete democracy.

Abroad, the Persian Empire, founded by Cyrus the Great, had already absorbed all of Asia Minor and extended its sway over the Ionian Greeks. The year of Aeschylus' birth had been marked by the Persian conquest of Egypt, followed by that of Babylon. When he was twenty-six, the Ionian Greeks revolted against their Persian masters, were defeated and partially enslaved (494), after which the Persian power sought to extend its conquests to the Greek mainland. This attempt, repulsed at Marathon (490), was finally defeated at Salamis, Plataea, and Mycale (480–79). The Greeks in turn, under the leadership of Athens, liberated the Ionians from Persian control and established the Confederacy of Delos to preserve the liberty thus gained.

By degrees, this alliance was transformed into the Athenian Empire, governed by an ascendant and confident democracy, under the leadership of many eminent men, none more so than Pericles, whose political power lasted from about 460 to his death in 429. The empire, though supported as a defense against Persia, became the natural target of disaffected allies, who found themselves becoming subjects, and of the jealousy of other Greek states, notably Sparta and Corinth. In 432 a Peloponnesian coalition under Spartan leadership opened hostilities with Athens, ostensibly to free Greece from her yoke. The war lasted, with an interval of armistice, till 404, when Athens, exhausted and over-extended by commitments, lost her last naval protection and was besieged and captured by the Peloponnesian forces.

Within the two years preceding this event, Euripides and Sophocles had both died. The works of the three dramatists were therefore composed during an expansive age in which democracy at home was matched by imperialism abroad. The repulse of the foreign invader was followed by the extension of Athenian commerce and influence throughout the eastern Mediterranean, and to some extent in the west also. This brought in the revenues and also encouraged the confidence in leadership which supported Pericles' ambitious policies and adorned the Acropolis with those public buildings, unmatched in purity of style, which still stand there.

But before the last plays were written, the strain of an exhausting and demoralizing war with fellow Greeks was beginning to tell, and in a moment of crisis even the democratic constitution had been called in question (411). For Aeschylus, his city's history had been an unbroken success story. In the lifetime of his two successors, she confronted an increasing series of problems, military, political, and social, which proved too much even for her energies to sustain.

4. GREEK THEATRICAL PERFORMANCE

The twelfth chapter of Aristotle's *Poetics* contains the following statement:

> . . . The quantitative sections . . . into which a tragedy is divided are the following: *prologos, epeisodion, exodos,* and the choral part, itself subdivided into *parodos* and *stasima.* These occur in all tragedies; there may also be actors' songs and *kommoi.*
>
> The *prologos* is that whole section which precedes the entrance of the chorus; the *epeisodion* is a whole section between complete choral odes; the *exodos* is that whole section of a tragedy which is not followed by a choral ode. In the choral part, the entrance song (*parodos*) is the first complete statement of the chorus, a *stasimon* is a song of the chorus without anapests or trochees; a *kommos* is a dirge in which actors and chorus join. . . .*

Students in English literature and other fields are likely to have been introduced to this famous passage. Yet scarcely any statement about Greek drama has caused more misunderstanding. It is schematic when it should be tentative, and definitive when it should be approximate. It has encouraged the presumption, widely held, that Greek plays were constructed according to a standard model from which, to be sure, the dramatist might diverge on occasion, but which nevertheless was his model. A prologue was followed by a choric entrance, for which anapests were supposedly the normal vehicle, and this by dialogue divided into episodes separated by full choruses, and concluded by an exit after the last chorus. No doubt the anonymous author (Aristotle could scarcely have been so dogmatic or so wrong) reflects those standards of mechanical formalism current in the period of the drama's decline. The key statement, "These occur in all tragedies," is false. The suggestion that actors' songs and *kommoi* (duets, trios, and quartets) were additions to the standard form is equally false. In Aeschylus alone, the reader will discover that neither his *The Persians* nor his *The Suppliants* has either

* Translation by G. M. A. Grube, from *Aristotle on Poetry and Style.* New York: Liberal Arts Press, 1958.

prologos or *exodos* (applying these terms as defined in the *Poetics*). If the *Prometheus Bound* has a *parodos*, it is technically a *kommos*, that is, a duet shared between Prometheus and the chorus. Two of the *stasima*, or choric odes, in *The Eumenides* are interrupted by nonchoric iambics. It would be interesting to know how the author of these remarks would apply his definition of *exodos* to *Agamemnon*. On his terms, the *exodos* extends from lines 1035 to 1673, but it includes one elaborate lyric duet sung by Cassandra and chorus, then the murder of Agamemnon, then an equally elaborate duet sung by Clytemnestra and chorus. The *parodos* of *The Seven Against Thebes* is not in anapests, nor is that of *The Eumenides*, and the *exodos* of *The Eumenides* is, in effect, an elaborate lyric trio shared between Athena and two different choruses.

No doubt the practice of Sophocles encouraged schematization, but even his practice often included in the *exodos* the climactic portions of the drama. *Oedipus the King* is an example. The practice of Euripides often reverts to the fluidity characteristic of Aeschylus. The fact seems to be that the whole conception of a tragedy as consisting of quantitative parts is erroneous, and the reader is best advised to approach each play as, in some sense, a new creation. Hence, though translators in this series may from time to time use the classic, or neoclassic, terms of the *Poetics*, they may equally be forced to apply modern terminology and speak of choric or lyric songs, of acts and scenes, of entrances, exits, and finales, according as the specific structure of any given play may require.

The conditions of production have never since been duplicated, and since they affect the way the plays were written, a word about them is in order. Performances took place in the open air. The audience sat on benches inserted into the slope of a recessed hillside. Chorus and actors shared not a stage but a circular dancing floor, on which the audience looked down. Thus, the Greek play remained a spectacle for the eye, as well as a verbal and musical delight to the ear, particularly as the figures executed in the dances produced patterns which an elevated angle of vision could appreciate. The audience was rarely asked to imagine the action as taking place in a closed room. Forecourts and courtyards and the street itself predominate as settings under the Mediterranean sky, and that sky itself, as the reader will discover, is never very far away from the characters' thought and speech.

At the back of the dancing floor stood a temporary wooden structure, the proscenium, with a central and two side doors and a flat roof. The doors were used for entrances and exits, the roof as a platform for appearances that called for an elevated position (those of gods, and sometimes human beings like the Watchman in the opening scene of *Aga-*

memnon). Behind the proscenium the actors could change their costumes, which were formalized to indicate sex, age, and social status. It is important to distinguish the *characters* who appear in a given play from the *actors* who played their parts. The former, while few by Shakespearean standards, considerably outnumbered the latter, who were rationed to two in some plays, three in most (four occasionally and doubtfully). The practical effect was that not more than two or three speaking parts could be carried on at any one time, so that at least some of the characters had to be played by different actors at different times, and the actors, relying on costume changes, had to be prepared to change their roles with rapidity. This ancient convention had an important result: The personality of the actor was severed from the role he played—this was also an effect of his mask—and reduced in importance (that is, until conventions changed in the Hellenistic age); and hence the burden of dramatic emphasis had to be carried entirely by the language, whoever happened to be speaking it. This is one reason why the verbal virtuosity of Greek tragedy has never been surpassed, even by Shakespeare.

The limitation of actors to two or three was undoubtedly related to a practical necessity. To examine (as one can do very easily in the typography employed in this series) the proportions of lyric to dialogue in a Greek play—that is, of sung to spoken parts, as these are assigned to individual actors (ignoring the chorus)—is to discover that the actors, and not just the chorus, had to have excellent singing voices enabling them to sustain solos, duets, trios and quartets. Even if they were assigned on a trial basis—the precise details of selection are disputable—the supply of suitable voices would be limited, and would require rationing among several plays competing simultaneously.

The standard phrase to describe authorship was "to teach a chorus," while "to grant a chorus" indicated the procedures of acceptance which put a play in production. Both seem to argue for the priority of the chorus in the classic Greek conception though the degree of priority is again a matter of dispute. The assembling and training of a group of singers and dancers (the total number is in dispute and may have varied) obviously took the most time, money, and skill. The expense was borne partly by the state and partly by private patrons, though the arrangements changed somewhat in the course of time. The playwright became his own producer, exercising a degree of control which is reflected in the tight unity of most Greek plays, exhibiting as they do something of the symmetry of Greek architecture.

The lyrics were accompanied by woodwinds, and the anapests, trochaic tetrameters, and dactyls were chanted, very possibly to the accompaniment of strings. The term chorus, however, indicates not singers but dancers, just as the terms strophe and antistrophe (which are Hellenistic), attached to symmetrical stanzas, originally indicated the turns and counter-turns of symmetrical dance patterns. This reminds us that, besides the music, we have lost the choreography, which was executed in figures of varying complexity. Conventions which today we would assign to ballet, opera, and oratorio are in Greek drama combined with a series of speaking parts to make something that we call by analogy a stage play, but which in fact is an ensemble uniquely Greek and classical and somewhat alien to modern expectations. It is a mistake, as any reader of *Agamemnon* or *Hippolytus* will discover, to think of plot as being restricted to the speaking parts. Lyric and dialogue are partners in the task of forwarding the action and exposing character and motive.

Though the place of performance of most but not all of these plays was the Theater of Dionysus on the southeast slope of the Acropolis and though one major occasion for the competition was the festival of the City Dionysia, this connection with the god and his cult—contrary to some widely held opinion—seems to have left no perceptible mark on the plays we have. *The Bacchae,* which might appear to be an exception, was not composed originally for performance in Athens, and its setting, we should note, is Theban. Even the Theater of Dionysus itself had replaced a more primitive arrangement in the market place. Furthermore tragic competitions were not restricted to the Dionysia. Latterly at least, they were also offered at the spring festival of the Lenaea. The link between Dionysus and the Greek theater became intimate in the Hellenistic age; their relationship in the sixth and fifth centuries is a matter of dispute, and was possibly somewhat fortuitous. Three prizes were awarded for first, second, and third places, and though special judges were selected for this purpose, they made their decision in front of the audience, which did not hesitate to register its own preferences. Thus the plays were composed for the Athenian public, not for an esoteric minority. Appeals to contemporary feeling on political and social issues are certainly not to be excluded on a priori grounds as violating the purity of Greek art. The reader himself will note without learned assistance how frequently a plot or episode manages to exploit Athenian pride and patriotism.

These original conditions of performance, as we have said, helped to mould the character of the text. The simplicity of the early playing area prompted the use of "verbal scenery" (instead of props and physical effects) and a "program" of plot and characters incorporated in the diction, most of it in the "prologue." But the plays were then revived continuously for centuries, during which time the details of staging, costumes, masks, the formal rules of dramaturgy, the profession of acting, and the construction of the theater itself, were all elaborated and formalized, even to some extent "modernized." The reader should be warned that in current handbooks on the subject he is likely to encounter much which draws on testimonies from these later periods, and which cannot be authenticated for the simpler but more creative conditions of the fifth century B.C.

E. A. H.

ON THE METRES OF GREEK TRAGEDY

One difference between Attic tragedy and opera is the domination of words over music. The music was there, in the choral passages, perhaps in all passages other than pure dialogue. But the rhythm of the words controlled the music. This is clearly to be inferred from the *strophic* structure of the full choral ode. A *strophe*, an elaborate series of metric elements arranged in a complex and unique pattern, will be followed by an *antistrophe* which repeats that pattern precisely, a long syllable in the one will match a long syllable in the other, and a short will match a short. This would be unthinkable as much in modern operatic forms as in medieval chant, where syllables can be lengthened or shortened, or can receive varying stress, as the rhythm of the music requires.

Greek metre depends on an alternation of long and short syllables, and not, as in English verse, on a sequence of stressed and unstressed syllables. In the main, there were three types of metre. First, in the dialogue, and in such passages as the spoken prologue and messengers' speeches, we have an iambic metre probably unaccompanied by music. It is called iambic trimeter because it can be best analyzed into three dipodies of two iambs each. There is a good analogy here with English blank verse, although the Greek line had six iambs rather than five as in English, and although the Greek line was stricter than the English analogue; in Greek comedy a good reader can instantly pick out a quoted or a parodied tragic trimeter from the surrounding comic trimeters by the greater regularity of the former. A typical line is 1. 12 of *Oedipus the King*:

> hŏ pāsĭ klēi|nŏs|| Ōidĭpūs| kălūmĕnōs
> the famous man whom all men know as Oedipus

where the single vertical represents the metrical division into dipodies, the double vertical the regular *caesura,* or word-ending within the third or fourth iambic foot.

When the chorus enter the orchestra in the *parodos,* again when they leave in the *exodos,* and in other passages, such as the introduction of new characters after a choral ode, the chorus, or one of the main characters, often speak in anapests. This metre can be arranged in lines, but in fact falls into *systems,* or long sequences, since there is no real metrical break at the end of the conventionally arranged lines. The series of anapests, that is, simply goes on until a shortened foot, a single syllable, coinciding with a verse-pause, ends the *system.* Thus we get ⏑⏑– ⏑⏑– . . . . . ⏑⏑– –. This is clearly a marching rhythm, and was usually accompanied by linear movement (on or off stage) by chorus or actors. Though some variations are allowed, spondees (– –) or dactyls (–⏑⏑) sometimes replacing the anapests (e.g., ⏑⏑– | – – | ⏑⏑– | –⏑⏑ | ⏑⏑–, etc. is possible), the anapestic is the steadiest, most driving, metre in Greek drama. Musically, it was probably between dialogue and choral song, probably accompanied by a simple melody and chanted rather than spoken, in a manner somewhat like *recitative.*

The full choral ode is an elaborate metrical, musical, and choreographic structure. In a modern English text, these odes often look like what used to be called *free verse.* They are in fact extremely tight structures, as the correspondence between strophe and antistrophe reveals. They are like free verse only in that each ode is a metrically unique creation: The metres are made up of known elements, but these elements are arranged into a pattern peculiar to the single ode.

The metrical structure of choral odes requires a book for adequate description. But three common types of metrical elements in them can be noted here. First *iambic:* here we have usually varied and syncopated iambic forms, appearing as short metrical cola, or sections; for example,

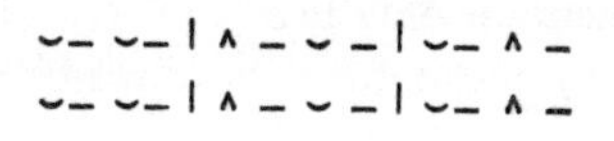

where the caret shows the missing syllable which would have made each of the three parts of these two cola (appearing as *lines* in our text) a standard iambic dipody. This metre is crisp and lively and relatively uncomplicated. In origin, it is closer to speech than other choral metres: In the hands of Aeschylus, it could reach (as in the choral odes of *Agamemnon*) an unparalleled religious and dramatic solemnity.

The favorite choral metre of Sophocles was the Aeolic (so-called because it appears in the lyric poetry of the Aeolic poets Sappho and Alcaeus) composed of elements which appear to be expanded choriambs (–⏑⏑–) with various combinations preceding and following them. The most common element is the glyconic – ⏑ – ⏑⏑ – ⏑ –; but endless variations are possible. It is perhaps the most mellifluous, and the most capable of subtle modulation of all choral metres. Sometimes iambic elements, and these sometimes in the form of a series of short syllables, will be introduced with great dramatic effect in an Aeolic sequence; and sometimes the Aeolic metre will be turned to the rapid and epic movement of a dactylic sequence (–⏑⏑ –⏑⏑. . .). Both these variations occur, for example, in the great first stasimon of *Antigone* (332 f.).

The wildest and most eccentric metre is the *dochmiac*, which seems to consist of staccato and abruptly syncopated iambic elements, typical forms being ⏑– – ⏑– and ⏑⏑⏑ ⏑⏑⏑–. This metre is used to mark statements of great fear or grief. The *parodos* of *The Seven Against Thebes*, where the Theban women imagine their city taken, is an extended passage in dochmiacs. Another example is *Hippolytus*, 811 f., where the chorus lament the suicide of Phaedra. Here as often in dochmiac, lines of iambic trimeter, as in spoken dialogue, are interspersed (813, 819–28, etc.). This may correspond to a break in the music and dancing, a further dramatic representation of extreme anxiety.

These choral or sung metres are most often uttered by the chorus, but sometimes by a single character, in a monody, or more often, in a lyric dialogue with the chorus. This latter is called a *kommos*, literally *(self-) striking* or *lamentation*, because that is the usual mode of such passages. By its nature, the kommos is often in dochmiac metre.

These are three of the principal metrical forms in choral song. Each has its distinct *ethos*, or emotional tone; and this distinct emotion was elaborated and enhanced by the dancing as well as the music, both these parts of the overwhelming choral performance being composed so as to correspond to the metrical pattern.

Sometimes more special metres are used in choruses for more special effect, and we shall mention only two: (1) The chorus at the beginning of *Agamemnon* as they move from their marching anapests into song begin with a dactylic hexameter –⏑⏑ –⏑⏑ –⏑⏑ –⏑⏑ –⏑⏑ – –, the metre of Homeric epic: that is clearly a deliberate recalling of the Homeric situation; (2) much of the *parodos* of *The Bacchae* (e.g., 64 ff.) is in an Ionic metre ⏑⏑– – ⏑⏑– –, etc. That is because this metre was used in ritual hymns to Dionysus.

Finally, we should note the trochaic tetrameter –⏑–⏑ –⏑–⏑ –⏑–⏑ –⏑–. A rapid and slightly rollicking form, this was said to be the original dialogue metre of tragedy, and its relative frequency in the early plays of Aeschylus may bear this out. It is a dialogue metre, is more formal than iambic trimeter, and expresses more hurry and agitation: e.g., *The Persians* 155–75, 215–48, where we note that for the Queen's long speech in 176–214, the metre reverts to the more conversational iambic trimeter.

The preceding is only a bare sketch of the intricacies, as well as the expressive possibilities, of Greek tragic metre. For fuller accounts (which, however, require some knowledge of Greek) see:

Oxford Classical Dictionary, article on *metre, Greek*, London: Oxford University Press, 1949.

D. S. Raven, *Greek Metre, an Introduction*, New York: Humanities Press, Inc., 1962.

W. J. W. Koster, *Traité de métrique grecque*, 2nd ed., Leiden: Brill, 1953.

ADAM PARRY

TRANSLATOR'S PREFACE

The translation is based in general on Gilbert Murray's Oxford Classical Text, second edition (OCT^2). Deviations from this text are noted in the commentary; they occur for the most part in lyric passages, some of which are so corrupt as to make certainty impossible. One basic variation concerns the ascription of parts in the latter part of the play; so far as possible I have excluded Antigone and Ismene, and have attributed the passages which Murray gives them to the Chorus; in many cases I am indebted to the suggestions of H. Lloyd-Jones (see Bibliography). For the version of the interchange between the Messenger and the Chorus in lines 803–13 I must be held responsible, though in this frequently discussed passage it may well be that my views coincide with those of other editors. In the actual translation I have tried to reproduce what the Greek says closely, but not with slavish literalness; this has involved an effort to reproduce metaphors and allusions where they do not seem grotesque and a careful attention to the emphases produced by word order. Where line references are made, they apply to the translation; but in most cases they match references to Murray's text.

My indebtedness to all who have advanced our knowledge of Aeschylus will be obvious to any reader and defies detailed acknowledgment. Specific acknowledgment is due, however, to my friend and colleague, Eric A. Havelock for his painstaking reading of my manuscript and his perspicacious and stimulating criticisms.

CHRISTOPHER M. DAWSON

INTRODUCTION

The play now known as *The Seven Against Thebes*[1] was the third play in a trilogy, which together with its satyr play, *The Sphinx*, was given first place at the Great Dionysia at Athens in the spring of 467 B.C. The first two plays were *Laius* and *Oedipus*. What was contained in these two plays is not clearly known; for although the legendary material, embodied earlier in a lost epic, the *Thebais*,[2] was popular and was used, for instance, by Sophocles in his *Oedipus the King*, *Oedipus at Colonus*, and *Antigone*, and by Euripides in his *The Phoenician Women*, the freedom with which Greek dramatists treated legendary characters and details of their story makes it useless to seek help from the plays I have mentioned. Comparison of *The Seven Against Thebes* with *Antigone* and *The Phoenician Women* or of *The Libation Bearers* of Aeschylus with the *Electras* of Sophocles and Euripides will show this at once. Some help may be given by references or possible allusions within *The Seven Against Thebes* itself to what preceded; and our one extant trilogy, the *Oresteia*, along with

[1] This name had become attached to the play by 405 B.C., when Aristophanes referred to it in his comedy, *The Frogs* (1021); yet the city attacked is never called Thebes in the play; it is the city of Cadmus and the Cadmeians. The dramatic and thematic importance of this emphasis on the city's founder will become obvious (see pages 19–22, and notes on pp. 19ff, *passim*). The original name of the play seems to be irretrievably lost; if we follow the pattern set by *Laius* and *Oedipus*, we might well suppose that it was called *Eteocles*.

[2] For the fragments of this epic, see Bibliography, s.v. Evelyn-White.

The Suppliants and *Prometheus Bound*, survivors of two other Aeschylean trilogies, may offer suggestions about the overall trilogic structure of which *The Seven Against Thebes* formed the last act.

To judge from *The Seven Against Thebes*, it seems likely that Aeschylus chose a simple and stark version of the Laius-Oedipus story. The trilogy may have presented—as is seen in the *Oresteia* and as is implied by *The Suppliants* and *Prometheus Bound*—a problem for which the first play offered a solution that served to present another problem for the second play; the second attempt at solution presented the problem that was resolved in the third play.[3]

The essential (and perhaps only) features of Aeschylus' drama are as follows: for some reason not given in *The Seven Against Thebes*, Laius, son of Labdacus, was told three times by the Delphic oracle (746–49)

> *thnêiskonta gennâs ater sôizein polin*
> "dying without children you save the city,"

a characteristically brief cryptic utterance, which confuses statement with command, but one which at least suggests that Laius' city would be safe if and when he had no descendants.[4] But in an act of folly Laius defied Apollo and produced a son, "disaster for himself, Oedipus who killed his father and seeded his mother's sacred soil, where he himself was reared" (751–54); the child was the result of "distracted frenzy" (757). In the hope of averting the oracular threat Laius exposed the child (still presumably unnamed), after piercing and fastening his feet together with some kind of clamp; the son grew up, and because of his physical affliction was known as Oedipus (Swollen-foot).[5] In early manhood he encountered a stranger at a crossroads at Potniae[6] and killed him. Coming

---

[3] Problems in the story of Laius and Oedipus that demand immediate attention are far too many to make any detailed reconstruction possible.

[4] The triple oracle may refer to three visits to Delphi and growing impatience on the part of Laius.

[5] This interpretation of the name, based on *oideô*, "become swollen," and *pous*, "foot," although implied elsewhere, is most clearly expressed in Euripides, *The Phoenician Women*, 26–27: "the child's ankles were pierced with iron spikes right through the middle; consequently the Greeks called him Oedipus, Swollen-foot." The same picture is found in Sophocles, *Oedipus the King*, 1036: "from this circumstance you were named what you are." See Bernard M. W. Knox, *Oedipus at Thebes* (New Haven: Yale University Press, 1957), page 182.

[6] This information is found in Aeschylus, frag. 173, in G. Murray's text (OCT²), page 201.

to the city of Cadmus later he found it in despair: the king was dead and the city was in the grip of a monster—the Sphinx, half-human and half-animal—which was devouring the inhabitants (775–77). Oedipus repulsed the Sphinx and, in reward for his services, was married to the widowed queen and became king of the city. In time he found out (778–84) that the man he had killed had been the king of the city, his own father, and that his wife was his mother. He thereupon blinded himself (while his mother-wife committed suicide).[7] We must assume that the rule of the city was subsequently taken over by Oedipus' sons, Eteocles and Polynices;[8] but apparently they neglected or mistreated their father, and in a fit of rage he uttered a curse on them: they should divide their property by steel and be left with only as much ground as is occupied by dead men (785–90, 730–33). After his death the brothers separated—the occasion is not stated; Eteocles remained as ruler of the city, while Polynices went into exile and persuaded Adrastus of Argos to gather and lead an invasion force against the Cadmeians.

When the play starts the city has been under siege for some time (21–22); but it is now in danger of a violent, desperate assault (28–29, 46–48) on each of the city's seven gates. The rest of the story is told in the play.

It should be noted that as far as *The Seven Against Thebes* is concerned, Apollo did not tell either Laius or Oedipus that if Laius had a son he would kill his father and marry his mother. These disasters did occur and are acknowledged in the play; but the prophecies of Apollo that are cited make no reference to them. Such references may have occurred in the preceding plays, but Aeschylus may have felt that the nature of the third play made them unnecessary and perhaps inimical to his purpose. In this play the fate of Laius' family is closely associated with the fate of his and their city; it is the family's survival or the city's that is involved. Parricide and incestuous marriage are things of the past; what matters is not a family but a city, not the past but present dangers. And Eteocles, devoted to his city and people but conscious of his family-inherited guilt, is a natural catalyst. Laius must die without descendants, said Apollo, if the city is to be safe; Laius did have descendants, so these must be removed if the city is to be safe. Eteocles is deeply concerned for the city's safety; but, apparently, he has not fully taken into account how deeply he himself is involved as a descendant of Laius.[9] First things first, is his

[7] For other versions of the Oedipus story, see Appendix A.

[8] See Appendix B.

[9] The character and motivation of Eteocles have been the subject of considerable discussion: he has been presented as a patriot who voluntarily

motto; defend the city, come what may. But he has not fully considered what "come what may" involves. Nor, indeed, has the Chorus, although it utters just such a prayer: "Zeus, at all costs ward off capture by the foe" (116–18). And when the choice has to be made, it is Eteocles who stands firm while the Chorus wavers (686–719). In accordance with Apollo's oracle it is the city, not the individual, that matters; the curse of Eteocles' father Oedipus makes the choice harder; to save the city Eteocles has to fight his own brother. This is where the emphasis of the third play lies; this is the climax to which developments lead; and, as will be seen, language and imagery concentrate on this aspect of the legend.

The boyhood and youth of Oedipus, the place of his upbringing, how he met and killed his father, what agreement (if any) had been made by the brothers, in what circumstances Polynices left the city—some of this must have been portrayed in the preceding plays. But gaps in a narrative are no hindrance to a playwright's presentation—witness the *Oresteia*. We must suppose that Aeschylus stripped his drama of all figures and concepts that might distract attention from the desired climax—salvation of the city by the heroic (even if curse-inspired) action of Eteocles and the elimination of Laius' "god-abhorred" family.

Eteocles, the central figure, is characterized at the start as a man who feels his responsibilities as leader of his city, who recognizes the fact that not all lies within his human control and that the rewards are not necessarily commensurate with his efforts, but who will nevertheless carefully make what he considers the appropriate decisions.[10] Such decisions

---

sacrificed himself to save his city (cf. Dawe, Lesky, and von Fritz), or at the other extreme, as a victim of "Necessity" or the Curse (cf. Solmsen; also Patzer and Wolff). Such extreme views find the play broken into two poorly harmonized sections, the break occurring at lines 653ff, where Eteocles decides to fight, even though he must fight his own brother. Wilamowitz suggested that Aeschylus had simply failed to reconcile two different epic sources; others (e.g., Patzer, Bacon) have suggested that Eteocles proceeded from a kind of blindness to realization of his position. It is, in general, difficult to reconcile the presentation of a hero who may be seen on two levels—as a devoted military commander and member of a curse-laden family (cf. Cameron) or as one whose choice to perform a noble act necessarily involves him in a crime. The article of Podlecki interprets Eteocles as "a bundle of contradictions"; Golden presents him as a self-interested power-seeker.

[10] In this Eteocles foreshadows Themistocles in Thucydides I. 138. 3: "Themistocles was a man . . . who by his innate perception . . . was most effective in judging what to do when a present emergency permitted little deliberation. . . . In fact, this man proved most effective in deciding on the spot what should be done." Eteocles also resembles Thucydides' Pericles in his views of a leader's rewards: "I am well aware that the plague

mark his whole behavior during the first 625 lines of the play, even when his patience has been sorely tried; in fact, it is this calculated responsible behavior that makes his final decision more ironic. Naturally he feels that the crew of his civic ship should show a similar sense of their responsibilities: all groups should devote themselves to the city's welfare. It is this sense of the need for civic responsibility that accounts in large measure for his violent attack on the Chorus of young women (182–202);[11] we have to wait for a Euripidean Jason or Hippolytus for any similar attack. But we must realize that these frantic young women, wrecking the morale of the city's inhabitants and defenders, may well bring about just what Eteocles has asked the gods to avert (69–77); all he is trying to do may be undone by the irrational emotions of women.[12]

Eteocles, who feels that armor, fearsome devices (397–406), and animal noises (475–76) cannot scare rational human beings, and who thinks that innocent reliance on the gods is not enough, is faced with problems created by women who have been driven by threatening noises into a terrified, unconstructive appeal to the gods. Only with difficulty, fighting both his own indignation and their emotions, does he bring them to any semblance of order. His violent criticism of the Chorus is not an attack on the gods to whom they appeal in panic, but an attack on the Chorus' ineffective and even destructive use of the gods and the powers the gods are supposed to have. True, some of his remarks have a cynical tone: god gets credit for success, man is blamed for failure (4–8, where the use of words appropriate to worship of the gods increases the irony: see commentary on 7); and there may be sardonic irony in his hope that Zeus the Protector will live up to his name (8–9); his suggestion of some kind of a *quid pro quo* relationship between gods and a city (77) is, however, reflected in the words of the Chorus later (304–20). Eteocles' interest is at this time primarily in the city's safety; the situation of the gods is incidental. He does not deny the existence of gods or some power or powers greater than man; and, indeed, although one detects sarcasm in his description of the blind seer ("king in his own realm," 27), he does accept his warnings about a desperate Argive assault; characteristically, however, it is the Scout's factual confirmation that rouses him to excitement and specific action.

---

has brought me still further unpopularity; but this is not fair, unless you are going to give me credit for any unexpected success, too. One should bear what heaven sends with resignation, but the actions of the enemy should be borne with manly heroism" (Thucydides II. 64. 1–2).

[11] For other possible reasons, see note on 182.

[12] Here, as in other respects, he resembles the Creon of Sophocles' *Antigone*.

Without doubt Eteocles recognizes the value of the gods and their cults for political and social coherence. Defense of their altars forms part of his civic appeal in lines 14–15, and on receiving the Scout's first report, he immediately calls on the appropriate orthodox deities while adding his personal religious anxiety (69–70); and he accepts the Chorus' right to offer worship to the gods (236), although he bids them be sensible in their emotional reactions.

The interchange between the Chorus and Eteocles (203–44)[13] and the following lines (245–86) show the difference between them clearly. The first four outbursts of the Chorus emphasize the fact that terror drove them in disorder to the gods' statues to seek and pray for protection; Eteocles insists on discipline and obedience and suggests that the city's walls are what will protect them, adding sardonically that the gods are said to abandon a captured city—a sentiment that harmonizes with his comment in lines 76–77. The Chorus asserts that there is a divine power that can rescue men from distress; but Eteocles firmly states, in what may be an ironic ambiguity, that it is man's job, not woman's, to act on offerings to the gods. The Chorus agrees that gods acting with men will provide good defense, and Eteocles admits their right to worship —but they must do it calmly, and he tells them to be ready for worse news, the death of men.

The last warning, coupled with more "noises off," rouses the Chorus to further excitement and more appeals to the gods; Eteocles' words and his assurance that he will handle the situation (248) seem to have had little effect; he has shown some spirit of compromise (236–38) but to no avail. It is hardly to be wondered at that he briefly loses his temper and then with deadly calmness brusquely orders them to keep quiet. His firmness must have impressed them, since they subside at once, though fearing the worst (263).

The emphasis on calmness in worship and a contributive religious attitude reaches a climax in lines 264–70, where Eteocles asks the Chorus to change their prayers: they are to ask the gods to help rather than merely to avert trouble; their appeals are to become paeans, prayers or chants for victory. He sets a pattern himself in a formal prayer and vow to the local deities, with promises of rewards for victory. Then, in revealing and characteristic fashion, he turns to action: he offers to serve him-

[13] The Chorus' excitement is expressed in lively lyric meters, which are sharply contrasted with the normal, almost cold, iambic trimeters of Eteocles. A similar lyric-iambic interchange occurs at 677–711, where the Chorus' excited efforts to dissuade Eteocles are contrasted with his rigid determination. See page 12 and notes on 203–44 and 677–719.

self as the seventh defender, to engage physically and prominently in the city's defense—in fact, because of the Chorus' irrationality, deserting his post as the ship's helmsman (208–10). So, in making what seems to be an appropriate immediate decision, he leads to his own downfall. This is, in essence, the overall picture of his activity in the play: his decisions, well calculated for the city's welfare, do save the city, but result in disaster for himself; and the warnings of Apollo are fulfilled—the city is saved and Laius has no descendants.[14]

The fact is that Eteocles takes a very pragmatic view of the gods; for him they seem to be useless without human action. He does not claim to know what the gods are or stand for; most of the time the word "god" or "gods" seems to represent luck or chance, or some undetermined power that gives good or bad luck. So in line 23 he says, "We have been lucky, thank god!" (although he immediately goes on to admit that the blind seer may be able to calculate what is unforeseen to many), and in line 35 he says, "God will give us luck!" (but he immediately notes that he has personally taken important steps to find out what the enemy is doing).

The crucial confrontation of the man of reason and action with stronger forces comes in the description of the Argive leaders in their warlike array and the choice of their opponents. After the Chorus' fearful picture of a captured city (287–368), the Messenger who reported the immediate threat of attack in lines 39–53 returns with specific information, giving a list of the attackers and the emblems on their shields; for each attacker Eteocles names a suitable opponent, and the Chorus adds a brief comment. In most cases Eteocles meets the threats and impiousness of the enemy by appropriate reference to the gods; but the first Cadmeian, Melanippus, is described rather as a noble hero who will act bravely to defend his motherland. Yet, for all his firm planning, Eteocles is by no means confident of success, since he admits that "Ares' dice," the chances of war, may determine Melanippus' fate. In view of this doubt, the emphasis on duty and responsibility with reference to possible disaster carries implications for Eteocles' own situation. The Chorus, shuddering and fearful, wishes that Melanippus may succeed with heaven's favor, and the Scout utters an "Amen," echoing the Chorus' "with heaven's favor"; his attitude in using the phrase is closer to that of Eteocles than to that of the Chorus.

Similar in tone is the Scout's apotropaic wish in line 426 as he describes Capaneus, who defies Zeus himself; the threats are sufficient to make him end his account in some doubt: just who will face such a

---

[14] On this disputed point, see pages 23–25.

braggart? But Eteocles is more confident; there is profit to be seen in the fact that the man already stationed at the second gate (448–49), Polyphontes, although no braggart, is as fiery as Zeus's thunderbolt and is favored by Artemis the Protector and other gods; Eteocles can, therefore, say *pepoitha,* "I am confident," "I know full well" (444). The Chorus' personal fears are too strong to permit confidence; they hope that Zeus's thunderbolt—not the man—will destroy the foe.

A colorless Eteoclus, the third attacker, has a shield that defies Ares, the war-god whose dice will decide the issue (469). In this case the Scout seems more confident; he does not doubt or ask questions, but asks Eteocles to send another champion of the quality of Polyphontes.[15] And Eteocles has just the man—in fact, he has already been sent[16]—Megareus, "from the Sown Men's breed" (474);[17] this man needs no gods to inspire him and prefers deeds to words; with a sense of duty to his kin like that of Melanippus, another of the Sown Men's breed (412–16), he will fight to the death if need be; and Eteocles ends rather with confident impatience than doubt (478–80). The Chorus remains prayerful.

With Hippomedon, gigantic like Capaneus, terror personified, a war-demented figure who has on his shield Typho, Zeus's enemy, Eteocles reaches his highest confidence; this enemy will have to face not only the city's goddess, Onca Pallas, and Hyperbius, a hero of outstanding worth, but a shield emblem perfectly suited to match that of Hippomedon—Zeus who blasted Typho and is an invincible god. It is important to note that the Cadmeian defender had already been picked (505), certainly for this very gate. But it is more important still to note that this particular choice seemed especially apt to Eteocles because he had, after all, been working in the dark: he did not know just who the seven enemy attackers were to be, and above all, he could not know which gate each would attack—that was determined by lot. Eteocles had to make his choices against the unknown; modified confidence marked his first assignment, Melanippus, already picked but not necessarily posted; the next two choices—men already stationed or sent to their posts—had proved fortunate; this fourth one is almost too good to be true. It is not surprising that Eteocles cries out, "Hermes made a shrewd match" (508); here reasoning and good luck have combined to meet the irrationality of the

---

[15] His word *pherenguon,* "one you can trust" (470) picks up Eteocles' *pherenguon,* "sure defender" (449).

[16] See note on 472.

[17] On the Sown Men and their importance in the play, see pages 19–22.

lot. Everything points to success,[18] and the air of confidence permeates even the Chorus, whose lyric utterance now begins with *pepoitha*, "I firmly believe" (521).

This is the high point of confidence; from here on there is a change —at first gradual, then sudden. The next attacker, Parthenopaeus, utterly impious, devoted to action, relying on his spear instead of gods, brings the threat nearer home, especially by his choice of shield emblem—the Sphinx that had done so much harm to the Cadmeians; he is, besides, confident (*pepoithôs*; cf. the Chorus in 521). Moreover, although not a native Argive, he feels a debt of nurture to the land that adopted him (548). Eteocles is driven to wish that the gods would turn the enemies' threats back upon the enemies themselves. But, as usual, he notes the practical aspect: he has a man of deeds, not words, Actor, who will hold off both Parthenopaeus and the Sphinx. His last words here, however, are not so confident (562). The Chorus is again shocked into terror (564); perhaps it is not merely Parthenopaeus' impiousness that terrifies them, but also the fact that one so young—not far from their own age—could be so savage. Dramatically, their imprecation foreshadows the fate of the next attacker, Amphiaraus.

This man was mentioned briefly in lines 378–79 and 382–83 (as interpreter of omens before attack). Wise and brave, marked by the four cardinal virtues according to Eteocles (610), he fully disapproves of the expedition[19] and attacks its two chief instigators, the war-crazy Tydeus and Polynices, who is violating his native land. But now, committed, he goes ahead, although he is aware that he must die. His lack of a shield emblem distinguishes him from his impious fellows. Eteocles here faces a problem: as the Scout has implied, if impious foes are dangerous, what of those who are devout (596)? One might expect the gods, whatever they may be, to punish those who defy them; but here is a god-fearing man who must also perish. Human existence seems to be utterly irrational; fate seems at times to be irresponsible, undiscriminating. How can a leader choose anyone to face such a god-fearing hero who, in spite of his piety, is doomed to death? Nevertheless, the gate has to be defended; so the active warrior Lasthenes is assigned to defend the sixth gate. Eteocles is again in some doubt: the last words of his comment on Parthenopaeus were not fully confident; now he sees that there is no guarantee that any

[18] This is the implication, whatever reading one accepts here. See note on 515.

[19] He had been tricked into it. See note on 568.

man, virtuous or not, can be successful (625); the climax in this developing attitude comes in the last words he utters in the play (719).

The Chorus' wish for the enemies' destruction by Zeus's thunderbolt before they reach the city or at least after repulse from the city (629–30) is a worthy epitaph-like tribute to Amphiaraus, who was swallowed up by the earth when it was opened by Zeus's thunderbolt to save him from a human pursuer.

A brief detail of the dramatic movement of concentration on the plight of Eteocles is indicated in lines 617–19: the words of Loxias are of tremendous importance to Eteocles' family, and the "god who keeps quiet or speaks to the point" is peculiarly understandable to the leader who feels that his duty is to make right decisions (1) and that silence is better than demoralizing outcries (262).

The Scout introduces the seventh attacker almost as if he were present,[20] without naming him, merely as "your own brother." The attacker makes threats but is not blasphemous; he calls upon his ancestral gods and demands what he considers his rights, and his shield displays Justice calmly guiding an exile, as it is claimed, to his proper home. The choice of defender is clearly a vital one, and the Scout squarely challenges Eteocles: "You are the one to choose; I've done my best to inform you," and then breaks off and almost in stammering fashion repeats himself: "You are the one, you are the captain," and departs (650–52).

Now, we know and the fifth-century Athenian audience knew that Eteocles had to confront Polynices; that was one element of the legend that a playwright could not change. But did the Scout know that the seventh defender was to be Eteocles? Did he realize what his account of the seventh attacker meant? I suggest that he did not know that Eteocles had promised to serve as the seventh defender; no hint of such knowledge is given by the Scout in his reference to Polynices in the preceding account (576–86); and what may seem to be a clumsy repetition in our text (650 and 652) may well be an indication of dismay on his part as he realizes what effect he is producing on Eteocles (and perhaps the Chorus) and remembers what all Cadmeians must obviously have known, the curse pronounced by Oedipus.

Did Eteocles know that Polynices would come next or, at least, did he realize that this was likely to be so? His violent exclamations in 653–55 suggest that he did not; yet one would have expected him to do so. True, the enemy's leader-in-chief, Adrastus, had not yet been mentioned as an attacker; Eteocles might well feel that as Cadmeian leader-in-chief,

---

[20] *tonde,* "this one here" (631).

it would be fitting for him to oppose Adrastus. But the Scout had spoken as if Polynices were as close to Amphiaraus in the field as was Tydeus; did this not arouse Eteocles' interest, especially since he, if anyone, knew his father's words? If the reference to his brother did not stir him, we can only suppose that his interest was concentrated on other matters; the fearful possibility of facing his brother is something that he must have pushed away and hidden in the recesses of his mind—deliberately pushed away, for he had clearly lived with the dreadful thought as his own nightmares show (710–11). Only once in this play, however, had the anxiety found words—in his solemn prayer for the city's welfare (69–73). It is here that the clue lies: Eteocles, the good captain, has consistently devoted his efforts to the welfare of the city and has consistently, perhaps hopefully, pushed aside his personal troubles. His outcry at the Scout's last account does not mean that he has suffered a sudden conversion of sorts,[21] but rather that he has finally realized that there are some things a mortal cannot escape.[22] All his careful planning cannot avert the vengeance summoned by his father's curse; he might try to disregard the curse, but simply not looking at it would not remove it. So we see him now and during the rest of the play like a prototype of the Creon of *Antigone*, who not only lost all that was personally dear to him, but above all found that what he most prided himself on, his patriotic and rational mind, had also failed him: "Everything I touched went askew," says Creon (*Antigone* 1344–45). Eteocles is in perhaps an even worse situation: what was apparently a perfectly accurate calculation reached a disastrously wrong answer.

His reaction to the Scout's account is characteristic: a brief emotional outcry, almost immediately checked as he reflects on the situation and what must be done. In his outcry he now links with his father's curse the hatred for his race felt by the gods, Apollo in particular, the

---

[21] See footnote 9.

[22] Not a rare thought in Greek literature. See, for instance, Callinus, frag. 1 Diehl, 8–9 and 12–15 (Edmonds, *Elegy and Iambus*, Callinus, frag. 1): "Death will come just at whatsoever time the Fates decide. Death is something that is ordained which no mortal shall escape, not even if he be descended from immortal forebears. He may often get safely away from battle and the clash of spears, but his appointed death comes on him at home"; or Simonides, frag. 12 Diehl (Edmonds, *Lyra Graeca*, vol. 2, frag. 68): "but death catches also the man who flees battle." See also Sophocles, *Antigone* 1337–38, quoted, page 13. The earliest statement of the theme is Hector's statement in *The Iliad* 6. 488: "But Destiny—nobody, I think, has escaped it."

god whose power was indicated earlier in 617–19 and will be emphasized by Eteocles in 689–91. The point is driven home later by the Chorus, especially in 800–802 (cf. perhaps 855–60). Soon the "ship's captain" and the rationalist take over (656ff). Polynices' claims are considered step by step from the time of his birth and rejected as universally untenable (670–71). Thus Eteocles builds up a confidence (*pepoithôs*, "convinced of this," 672), which for him justifies his confrontation with his brother; the general confrontation of Argives and Cadmeians has resolved itself into a confrontation of brother with brother, foe with personal foe (674–75). Clarification of the situation once reached, Eteocles immediately prepares for action (675–76) and demands his weapons and armor. Nothing will deter him; the Chorus' plea that he avoid the pollution of kindred bloodshed merely evokes the statement that if one must die it should be as a hero.

This is a critical moment, and it is marked by another lyric-iambic interchange[23] in which the Chorus urges Eteocles, in phrases of rich metaphorical content, to resist his impulse to face Polynices; they suggest that the avenging Fury will leave the family if appropriate sacrifices are paid to the gods. Resistance is not possible, says Eteocles; Apollo has condemned the whole family of Laius to Cocytus (underground River of Wailing), and the curse is irrevocably settled on him. The suggestion of the Chorus that caution, wise retreat, and sacrifice to the gods may avert disaster meets with a disillusioned answer: "Gods? all they want is my blood, fulfillment of their oracles; and as for averting disaster, I should have known—I had nightmares enough to warn me—that this split would come."

There is a quick close to the scene—eight iambic lines (712–19), in which Eteocles' character and position are clarified: he bids the Chorus be brief (he still prefers action to talk)and in spite of their appeals that he should not go to defend the seventh gate and risk shedding his brother's blood, and although they assert that the gods will accept a victory even if he personally draws back, he refuses to withdraw; his mind is made up; to withdraw would be unheroic, and besides, "When god gives evil, man cannot escape" (719).

These are Eteocles' last words: no long soliloquy like that of Hector facing Achilles before Troy (*Iliad* 22. 99–130); no concept of self-sacrifice for his city, although the city's welfare has been foremost in his thinking; no abject surrender; no collapse like that of Creon in *Antigone*, who asked to be led away—now a mere nothing or less than nothing,

---

[23] See above, page 6 and footnote 13.

while the Sophoclean Chorus said what Eteocles might have said here, "Prayer is useless, for mortals have no escape from what is destined" (1337–38). Eteocles is defeated, personally, as an individual, utterly, absolutely; the reasoning mind of man has been overcome by the irrational, the incalculable, and thus the unavoidable, by the Fury, the avenging power evoked by the oracle of Apollo, reawakened and continued by the curse of Oedipus, and indeed by Eteocles' own invocation in line 70. He realizes this, but in true heroic tradition is determined not to run; doomed he may be, but he will salvage whatever honor he can from the shipwreck of his plans. Like Henley's *Invictus* he has an unconquerable soul, whatever gods there be.[24]

This long discussion of Eteocles is out of line with his own instructions ("be brief," 713); but he is, after all, the one real figure in the play. He is the last of three human instruments that show the working of the divine will: Laius who disobeyed the gods rashly and with foreknowledge; Oedipus who committed error, perhaps rashly and perhaps with forewarning; and Eteocles, who may have committed no sin but disregarded or perhaps failed to understand warnings and put the safety of his country first. One argues *ex silentio* here, but we may well have three differentiated characters: Laius who set personal desires above his city's welfare; Oedipus who benefited his city but brought ruin on himself; Eteocles who deliberately set his city's welfare first, even though he came to realize that it meant disaster for himself.

Until the end of the play Polynices is seen only through the eyes of people more or less hostile. According to the Scout (576–86), Amphiaraus, stationed next to Polynices, attacked him for his impiety and his violent unpatriotic behavior, with significant metaphorical connotations. The Scout himself (631–48) is somewhat less vicious, portraying an angry exile demanding what he thinks are his rights and just requital. Eteocles regards him as an utter villain. The Chorus says nothing about him until Eteocles has determined to face him, merely reacting to the fear that Eteocles may slay or be slain by his own brother. In what may be called the longer version of the play (see pages 22–24) the Herald pronounces him a traitor condemned by the city government, but Antigone swears to bury him, without any real defense of his behavior, and she is followed apparently by half the Chorus.

Polynices claims his right (645–48), whereas Eteocles denies that he ever had any (662–69). The play itself gives us no information on this matter; we do not know whether one brother was older than the

[24] See pages 11–12.

other or whether they were twins (although the constant emphasis on duality and birth from the same womb might incline one to think so); we are not told why Eteocles refused to allow Polynices to hold power in the Cadmeian city; if we can believe Polynices' claim, he was deprived of his rights and banished by Eteocles;[25] if we believe Eteocles' words, his brother fully deserved such punishment.[26] Significantly, nowhere in the play is any reproach hurled against Eteocles, even by the panic-stricken Chorus; although they may be dubious about his attitude toward the gods, they still regard him with respect and even affection. For the purposes of this play Aeschylus found the legal details—as he did Creon or the name of Oedipus' mother—inconsequential.

The Scout requires little comment. He is clearly a faithful reporter, impressed by pageantry and inclined to florid description; he is probably a man after Eteocles' own heart in his emphasis on personal participation and on accuracy of information that will result in safety.[27] He must be typical of the Cadmeian people in his respect for Eteocles as the head of state; he regards him as competent and able to seize an opportunity or meet a crisis,[28] and when the pressure becomes intense he is only too glad to leave the matter in Eteocles' hands.[29]

About the Chorus, whose part occupies more than half the play, much has been said already and more will be found in the commentary; but further comment is appropriate here.

A primary function of this Chorus is to form a clear-cut background for Eteocles, both to show his immediate practical civic difficulties and to reveal the significance of the evil destiny of Laius' family, which has come to involve Eteocles. The early excitement of the Chorus is replaced in the middle of the play by the ceremonial description of the Argive attackers and Eteocles' answers; the Chorus is restricted to brief prayerful or imprecatory lyric utterance. In the ensuing lyric-iambic interchange[30] it is the Chorus that tries to quiet an excited Eteocles—although since Eteocles speaks in iambic trimeters he is presumably more determined than excited.

Fear is the tone of the choral ode that follows Eteocles' departure; the Chorus is recalled from personal terrors to remembrance of the curse uttered by Oedipus, the warning of Apollo to Laius, and the conse-

[25] 637–38; cf. 647–48.
[26] 662–71.
[27] 41, 66–67, 375, and 40, 67–68.
[28] 62–64, 65; cf. Eteocles himself in 1–3.
[29] 650–52.
[30] See above, page 6 and footnote 13.

quences; it fears that the brothers will die and that their deaths may involve the city in ruin. Some reassurance about the city comes from the Messenger, but the Chorus remains uneasy as late as lines 843–44; then its fear is transformed into doubts about whether there should be joy at the city's safety or sorrow at the deaths of the princes. The Chorus divides into two groups, one lamenting Eteocles, the other Polynices. In their lyrics of lament they dwell on the fulfillment of Oedipus' curse, with a brief reference to the unhappy (unnamed) mother who bore the sons, and end with a firm statement of the end of the intrafamily feuds with the triumph of *Âtê*, "Sinful Folly," and the house's evil fortune (953–60). Lament continues in a lyric-iambic interchange between two groups or two speakers with full choral refrains, and the division into two groups persists to the end of the play as we have it. In the final anapaestic passage (1054–78) the panic that the Chorus felt at the start has disappeared; it is replaced by awe at the power of the avenging Fury and by sorrow for the two princes; it is especially fitting that the last words should be a splendid tribute to the captain who has saved his vessel from shipwreck (1075–78).

The Chorus portrays the enemy emotionally in its reaction to the Argive chariots and horses, the spearmen, and the slingers; the Scout gives a detailed description of seven men, prominent warriors like the Cadmeian "finest men, the city's choice" (57). An animal quality ascribed to them metaphorically in line 53 persists as the Scout begins his account. Tydeus, battle-hungry like the lions of line 53 (380), is depicted in animal terms (381–82, 393–94) and seeks to inspire terror by bizarre accoutrements. Gigantic Capaneus is blasphemous (427–31). Eteoclus, blasphemous too, but somewhat colorless, has horses whose attitude and equipment recall Tydeus (461–64). Another giant, Hippomedon, is possessed by demonic fury (497–98). The fifth attacker, Parthenopaeus, though impious, is of less formidable aspect; but his beauty of form is belied by the savagery of his disposition, and his emblem, the Sphinx, is a calculated insult; he is, however, at least a human being, and serves to prepare for the next man, Amphiaraus. This pre-Socratic embodiment of the four virtues—wisdom, justice, piety, courage (610)—can hardly be called an attacker, His heart was not in the expedition; he had been tricked into it, but he observed his commitments even though he knew he would die. No braggart and with no emblem on his shield, he stands in sharp contrast to the monstrous figures who preceded him and to Polynices; his vigorous comments on Tydeus and Polynices serve to link the first and last of the attackers. Polynices, a man who wants to avenge himself on his enemy—an idea not strange to a fifth-century Greek—

is set off from the other attackers by the phrase "escorted quietly," which is applied to his shield-emblem (645). He is brought closer to Eteocles than any of the others, Amphiaraus excepted, as a human being rather than a brute.[31]

The mighty, avenging curse of his father that was briefly mentioned by Eteocles early in the play (70) emerges later—when Eteocles finds that he is to fight his brother—as a far more serious opponent than his brother or the whole Argive force; worse still, the curse is the instrument or ally of an evil destiny settled on the family two generations earlier by an utterance of Apollo. Just what the paternal curse and Apollo's utterance were we are not told in this play until Eteocles has made all his own careful, rationalized preparations for the defense of his city, made all those right decisions that he declared so important for a city's leader. The holding back of this information contributes heavily to the isolation of and concentration on Eteocles as the heroic victim in this tragic dramatic movement.[32]

From the excited outburst of Eteocles on learning that he must confront his brother (653–55) and from the Chorus' dialogue with him (677–719), we gather that fighting with his brother over their inheritance and the probability of death formed part of Oedipus' curse.[33] Eteocles had lived in the shadow of this curse (709–11); the Chorus knew of it, as did the Messenger (815–19), but all had pushed it aside, disregarding

[31] One detail deserves attention. Although the attackers are called Achaeans (Eteocles, 28; the Chorus, 324), the Chorus also calls them men "with an alien tongue" (170); Eteocles describes Cadmeia as a city that speaks Greek and has established homes, is free, and should not be subjected to slavery's yoke (73–75); the Messenger later assures the Chorus that the city "has escaped slavery's yoke" (793). This is odd language to apply to warfare between Greek cities, but the oddness should not lead us into speculations about pre-Achaean and Achaean settlements or variations in Greek dialect. Every Athenian in the audience would know what the capture of a Greek city by a foreign, barbarian (non-Greek speaking), partly nomadic host could mean (cf. 321–68). Five years earlier Aeschylus had celebrated in *The Persians* Athens' noble answer to just such a possible disaster and had above all exploited the yoke-of-slavery image. The poignant memories offered a ready source of emotional response to which Aeschylus could appeal in this picture of a beleaguered city.

[32] We must remember that the tension that might be felt by a modern reader of this play would differ from that of the fifth-century audience who viewed the whole three-act drama; they would have heard the warning of Apollo and the curse of Oedipus uttered in some fashion in the earlier plays; their interest might lie in wondering just how Eteocles would be brought to realize the real problem facing him.

[33] Cf. 726: "child-destructive strife here presses on."

it in the city's peril. It is now brought into the open on Eteocles' departure for battle. From the statements of the Chorus (788–90, 907–10) and of the Messenger (816–19), we may get some idea of the actual words used: the brothers are to divide their property by an allotment decided by the sword; they will get enough land to be buried in (731–33, 818), but no great estates, although the earth will stretch endlessly beneath them (733, 949–50). The original curse may have been succinct and oracular; its wording permitted word-play on Greek forms meaning "allot" and "arbitrate" and "reconcile." [34]

The Chorus, however, does more than merely explain the curse of Oedipus; it relates the curse to the transgressions of Laius who disobeyed Apollo's warnings. "New evils are mixed with the old ones" (740–41); the father's curse evoked the ever-present Erinys, the avenging Fury (723, 886–87, 897–98), and now in the third generation the sin of Laius continues to afflict his descendants; a triple-crested wave has swept over the family (760).

The story of the complex interrelationship of the three generations —Laius and his wife, Oedipus and his mother-wife, and their sons Eteocles and Polynices—is portrayed in compressed form in 750–57 (see also 926–29). This past history rouses a double fear in the hearts of the Chorus, fear for Eteocles and Polynices and their primary fear for the city (764–65). The two fears are linked, and we may assume that when they speak of a swift fulfillment of Oedipus' curse in 790–91, they envisage threatening capture of their city. Even the Messenger's reassurance (792–98) does not remove their doubts (843–44); the god's warnings—not merely Oedipus' curse—"keep their edge." The visible evidence of the bodies of the cursed sons (848) shows that the curse and Fury have had effect. The family hated by Apollo (689–91; cf. 653) has been brought low; the victory of the Cadmeians is crowned not by a triumphant paean but by a sad procession in every respect at variance with the joy of a shining Apollo (854–60) and by a discordant chant sung by the *Arae*, the Curses, celebrating the victory of *Âtê*, Sinful Folly (953–56).[35]

The destructive power of the Fury was not merely unjustified supernatural malevolence; it was a retributional force aroused and assisted by the actions of human beings—Laius, Oedipus, and Oedipus' sons—and these actions were due to a kind of madness or foolish anger. Laius was led by "his own foolish counsel" (750) into an act of folly (802), into

---

[34] Cf., for instance, 914, *taphôn patrôiôn lakhai*, "burial in their father's lot," where *lakhai*, a rare word, may be connected with (and here reflect) both "digging" and "allotment."

[35] Cf. also the triumph of the Erinyes in 1054–56.

disobeying Apollo's warning (745–49, 842), and into a mad, frenzied mating (756–57). Oedipus' curse was the violent curse of a man distracted by realization of the horror of his marriage (678, 781), wildly demented (724–25, 786). The Chorus fears that Eteocles is in the grip of a "heart-consuming, war-craving folly and evil passion" (686–88), a "ravenous yearning" (692). He and his brother held "impious thoughts" (831), were misguided and heedless (875–76), and demented (892) in their mad rivalry (935). The whole family of Oedipus came to deserve the description "maddened by god and god-abhorred, all-wretched" (653–54).

Aeschylus is known for his use of pervading, dominant metaphors: timid doves fleeing before birds of prey in *The Suppliants;* the enslaving yoke in *The Persians*; the hunter who becomes hunted, the net or web, the red of blood and fire in the *Oresteia;* the fetters in *Prometheus Bound.* In *The Seven Against Thebes* we meet two: the ship of state and the complex picture of the motherland.

The picture of a leader as a ship's captain would be readily accepted by Greeks, few of whom lived very far from the sea, and especially by the nautically minded Athenians.[36] In *The Seven Against Thebes* Eteocles introduces himself as the careful captain of the Cadmeian ship of state (1–3); he wants an obedient, reliable crew (30–35); in view of the threatening storm, the squalls of Ares, the Scout calls on Eteocles' ability as a captain (62–65). This image rides firmly through the play with many related figures in its wake; one notes, for instance, the swelling of citizen chants in 7 and the white foam-flecks in 60. The Chorus sees its peril in terms of floods, booming waves, crashing torrents (79–86), whitecaps, and wind-whipped surges (114–15); the Argive horses' bits are "steering gear" (206–7); the Chorus becomes undisciplined, disruptive in its "foaming rushes" (191), positively mutinous, reluctant to rely on the captain (208–10); in the baleful storm the girls put their trust in gods and, in terms worthy of Archilochus,[37] hope that heaven may calm the storm and rescue them (227–29). They are finally brought to admit that the ship may actually be seaworthy.[38] The captain naturally describes his champions as "counter-oarsmen," *antêretâs* (282–83), and hopes to anticipate a rush of "foaming stories" (285).

---

[36] Related pictures are as old as Homer, where armies are depicted as advancing waves (*Iliad* 13. 381ff, 624ff): the stormy perils of war can be found in Archilochus, the troubles of the ship of state in Alcaeus.

[37] See note on 227.

[38] See note on 216.

With the re-entry of the Scout and the description of the attackers and their counterparts, the nautical metaphor disappears; the dramatic movement demands that the captain be isolated from his city until all interest is concentrated on him as the son of Oedipus, descendant of Laius—except at the very end of the Scout's description, when he realizes that his captain is facing a peculiarly significant storm: "you are the one to choose the proper course" (*nauklêrein*, "steer the ship," 652). Emphasis on the curse of Oedipus, Apollo's warning, and their effects on Eteocles and Polynices, third generation of Laius' family, precludes extensive use of the ship-of-state metaphor after the exit of Eteocles; but its influence is still felt. One significant passage comes in the middle of the last stasimon (758–63): Laius' transgression has resulted in a violent sea-storm which, the Chorus fears, threatens the ship of state—not merely the two princes—and only a city wall serves as bulwark.[39] The Messenger reports that the storm is over, the city's walls proved watertight, and the bulwarks stood firm (795–98),[40] though Eteocles and Polynices are dead. Later, if we accept an almost certain emendation (1009), Eteocles is described as his city's bulwark,[41] and our text ends with a splendid tribute to the man who saved the city from shipwreck (1074–78).

Other passages less directly connected with the ship image, but influenced by the general wave-and-wind picture, include the destructive torrent of 360–62, the piling up of one wave of grief on another (368), the possible wind-change of Destiny (705–8), the forceful current of Oedipus' curse (819), the way in which Laius' family is swept off to the Cocytus (689–91), and the extraordinary unhallowed, sacred voyage of 855–60.

The second image or series of derived images is not extraneous, like the ship of state, but integral in the story of Cadmus and more significant in its relationship to *The Seven* and probably to the whole trilogy. The source of the metaphor is the legend of the founding of the Cadmeian city. While preparing to found his city Cadmus had to kill a dangerous serpent; he was then advised by Athena to sow the serpent's teeth in the ground. Immediately a crop of armed men sprang up and fell to fighting among themselves until only five were left; these men, *Spartoi*, "Sown Men," literally autochthonous, born of the soil, children of the

[39] See also note on 768.

[40] This is the point at which the new captain, Creon, begins in Sophocles' *Antigone* 162ff: his city again rides safe after much buffeting—to Creon's relief (note the final *palin* in 163, "safe again at last").

[41] See notes on 216 and 795.

same mother, founded the noble families of Cadmus' city. The end of the fratricidal strife is no doubt reflected in the legend that Cadmus married Harmonia, daughter of Ares and Aphrodite.

The first defender, Melanippus, is a scion of the Sown Men, and Eteocles asserts that *dikê homaimôn*, "duty to his kin, the rights of consanguinity" demands that he protect his motherland (412–16); the third defender, Megareus, is of similar stock, and he will repay his land the debt he owes it for nurture (*tropheia*) even if it means his death (477). Reference of this obligation of a child to his parents and its specific application to Cadmeian citizens was made early in the play, immediately after Eteocles' picture of himself as the state's captain (10–20); the metaphor is introduced unobtrusively in "ripe maturity" (almost a cliché); it is continued in "cherishing . . . your body's growth" and in "life's prime season"; with the phrase "the motherland, a nurse most dear" we begin to see the picture clearly; the earth is a mother who has lovingly and unstintingly devoted herself to the nourishing of her human offspring, from the time when they were tiny and crept on the ground like crawling plants that derived their sustenance from the soil.[42] The Cadmeians are children of the land, and the motherland may well expect repayment for her care. This justifies Aeschylus' statement later (901–2): "the ground that loves her sons laments."

Foster mothers, too, are entitled to this repayment; Parthenopaeus (548) is "an alien repaying Argos for nurture."

Eteocles and Polynices, like the original fratricidal Sown Men, born from the same mother, each destroying the other, spilled their blood on Cadmeian soil (821). The hatred between them came to an end (937), but in a manner far different from the battle of the Sown Men; agreement was finally reached in that conflict before all were killed, but here the hatred was ended only when both sons of Oedipus were destroyed and their blood was mingled with the earth and with each other's blood (937–40; cf. 736–37).

Although Polynices was a son of the Cadmeian soil, his offense is not generally presented as one against the motherland. He is rebuked by Amphiaraus for attacking *polin patrôiân*, "his father's town" (582);[43] in 668 Eteocles says that Polynices is ravishing his fatherland, and in

[42] This must be the connotation of *neous herpontas eumenei pedôi*, "young ones creeping on the kindly ground" (18–19).

[43] The figure on his shield, which claims to be *Dikê*, "Justice," asserts, "I shall restore this man; he shall have his father's city and home to move in" (647–48).

887 the Chorus grieves for him as one who attacked his father's house. Why this emphasis on *patrôios*, "belonging to one's fathers," and just what is the significance of lines 584–86?

> The mother-source—who can block that justly?
> and your father's land—if your ambition
> and spear take it, can it be your ally?

The answer to the question is to be found—as it should be in any coherent work of art—within the play itself. The clue lies in lines 752–56:

> Oedipus who killed his father
> and seeded his mother's
> sacred soil, where he himself was reared,
> accepting the bloody stock
> that grew.

As we read these words the link between the mother-source and the fatherland becomes clear. In producing Eteocles and Polynices, the unholy crop that destroyed itself, Oedipus sinned against the mother who bore him; but at the same time he committed a further offense against his father, the father whom he had already slain and whose place, home, and bed he had taken. Like Polynices (668) he ravished his father's land. In fact, for the discarded and unrecognized child of Laius most of Eteocles' comment on Polynices is equally applicable. It is surely significant that after the concise picture of the complex interrelationships of the three generations of Laius' family, the Chorus speaks of the fearsome triple-crested waves of destiny (758–61).[44]

A conclusion is reached, but it is a shocking conclusion: "ended now their hatred . . . now they truly share their blood" (937–40). Whose blood is shared? The blood of Polynices and Eteocles, of Oedipus and Jocasta, of Laius and Jocasta, of the motherland. The two sons have reached agreement in the bosom of the earth, the mother of Cadmeian heroes.[45] The brothers are truly *homaimoi*, "one in blood," one with one another, one with mother and their father-brother, and now one with the Sown Men and with the blood-enriched and blood-supplying motherland.

---

[44] Eteocles' comment in line 194, "we are ruined from within by our own," could be applied to the whole family history.

[45] They have passed to the land of the dead, a *pandokon kherson*, "a land which welcomes all" in indistinguishable darkness (860) and is as all-embracing as the hospitable earth that nurtured them (*pandokousa*, 17).

The motherland may well share in the sympathy expressed for the mother of Eteocles and Polynices (926–32); the lamenting land of lines 901–2 is a mother crying for her native sons. And when Eteocles and Polynices share their father's burial lot (914), ironically called later the most honorable place (1003), "buried in their own land's embrace" (1008), they will grievously be sharing their father's bed (1004).

Several passages reflect the influence of this earth-and-growth metaphor: the attackers' blood may be blended with the soil (48); Amphiaraus will enrich the Cadmeian land by being buried there (587–88); we may add Amphiaraus' fruitful thoughts (593–94), the fruit of Loxias' words (618), the evil growths that Actor will prevent (556–57), the bitter fruit of bloodshed (693), the utter extirpation of a city (71–72). More significant are the awesome crop that results from evil associations (599–601) and the razing of a city seen in terms of the ravaging of the earth's products (357–62).

THE ENDING OF THE PLAY

The last part of the play has been the subject of considerable discussion for more than a century. Until 1848 it was generally supposed that *The Seven Against Thebes* was the second play of a trilogy; ending with a question and looking forward to further efforts at a solution, it was eminently suitable as a transitional act in a three-act drama. But in 1848 there was published for the first time the *didaskalia*, i.e., a statement giving the writer and the names of a group of plays, the date at which the plays were exhibited, and the success won by the playwright. This statement from the most notable manuscript of Aeschylus, the Medicean, showed that *The Seven Against Thebes* was the last play in a trilogy that was awarded first place in 467 B.C. There was inevitable reexamination of the play and its appropriateness as a concluding act, and in the course of reexamination many details of language and poetic style that had hitherto been passed over were brought into question; but special attention was given to the content of the play and the obvious fact that with our present text, the trilogy must end without giving a solution; instead, it points to further troubles beyond the scope of the actual trilogy.

The dilemma may be seen if we consider the words of a scholar who edited *The Seven Against Thebes* only five years after the publication of the *didaskalia*: "A poet like Aeschylus, however crude and irregular his plots may occasionally have been, could never have committed so egregious an error as to leave his audience entirely in the dark about the fate of Antigone, after having excited their deepest sympathy in behalf of the heroic maiden by stating her determined opposition to the decree of the Cadmeian senate, and the awful doom which awaited her in case she should persist in her resolve of burying her outlawed brother. . . . We are, therefore, compelled, in the face of the statement of the Didaskalia (the genuineness of which is probably far from being firmly established), to believe that the "Septem" formed the second part of a trilogy, whatever the concluding play may have been." [46] I agree with the estimate of Aeschylus as a writer; I cannot accept the concluding statement. Nor can any serious scholar reject the evidence of the *didaskalia*. The answer accepted generally—by no means universally, however—is to regard much of the last fifth of the play as spurious, the interpolation of some producer or actors under the influence of Sophocles' *Antigone*; the most effective proponents of this view were Bergk and Wilamowitz, who cast suspicion on lines 861–74, 961–1004, 1005–78. The first passage introduces the two sisters, Antigone and Ismene; the second is a stichomythic lyric lament for the two princes; the third begins with an iambic conflict between Antigone and a Herald who forbids burial of Polynices and ends the play with a choral song, as the Chorus and actors leave with the bodies of Eteocles and Polynices.

It is most improbable that a trilogy could end so inconclusively as the Cadmeian trilogy must if we accept the present text.[47] Parallels for inconclusive endings noted as support for the text are drawn not from trilogies but from single plays that did not form part of a trilogy; the multiple unsettled questions of Euripides' *The Phoenician Women*, for instance, are enough for more than any three-act drama. It is true that we have only one complete trilogy preserved, the *Oresteia*; but it is most unlikely that *The Suppliants* trilogy and the *Prometheus* trilogy ended with unresolved questions; to suggest that *The Seven Against Thebes* might have ended with unresolved questions is a dangerous argument *ex silentio*, disregarding such evidence as we do have. It does not help to suggest—as some have—that Aeschylus may have had another trilogy in

[46] A. Sachtleben, *Septem contra Thebas* (Boston and Cambridge: James Munroe and Company, 1853), pp. vii–viii.

[47] An examination of the problem of the end of *The Seven Against Thebes* was made by H. Lloyd-Jones. His thoroughness makes it unnecessary for me to go through all the evidence adduced pro and con; I shall merely indicate the viewpoint from which the translation and commentary were undertaken and adduce a few significant details. R. H. Dawe's valuable review of Lloyd-Jones' views reached me after my manuscript was completed; much of what he says supports the views I have expressed here.

mind, a second multiple volume; to say the least, he could not guarantee its presentation.

In the text itself we have absolutely no suggestion before the suspect lines 861–74 that Eteocles and Polynices had any sisters; even after specific reference is made in lines 861–65, their names do not appear again in the text, and the manuscript attribution of lines to the sisters and, indeed, to the Chorus is scanty, chaotic, and improbable. Introduction of the sisters suggests a period in theater history when more than two actors were available to a dramatist and when the virtuosity of solo performers replaced the disciplined skill of the Chorus.

There are also indications that Aeschylus presented Eteocles and Polynices, who are themselves childless,[48] as the last of their family. In lines 690–91 Eteocles suggests that in his duel with his brother, the "whole Phoebus-hated race of Laius" will be destroyed. The brothers are described as "of the same seed . . . utterly destroyed" (933), in contrast with the Sown Men, who survived in part; and in the following lines, which lead up to what could well be a satisfactory finale, we find an emphasis on finality: strife is ended (936), hatred is ended (937); there is a sad victorious climax, victorious for the Curses and Sinful Folly, which have defeated the family of Laius in utter rout, so that the *Daimôn*, the destiny of the family, has reached its goal in conquest over the two princes.[49] The war is over. Such an interpretation gives more meaning to the phrases "the house-destroying god" (720–21) and "ruin of the house, Vengeful Spirits" (1054–55).

In this connection one choral passage, which at first seems like a gratuitous moral comment (766–71), becomes more pertinent. After expressing fears that the city may be laid low along with Eteocles and

[48] Especially significant is the phrase *ateknous klausô polemarkhous*, "am I to weep for leaders who are childless?" (827–28); no tortuous efforts to evade the obvious can make *ateknous* mean anything other than "childless." The only objection that can be found in the text to the idea that Eteocles and Polynices died without children is found in line 903: "their goods await followers" (*epigonois*). The word here translated "followers" almost inevitably suggests the next legendary attack on the Cadmeian city by the descendants of the original Seven; but it is the only such reference in the play and it could be part of a simple general comment: other people will take over their property. It seems to me important that any references, including this one, to future threats to the city come from the lips of the Chorus (764–65, 843–44); such comments are not made by the playwright *in propria persona*, but by a bunch of scared girls whose panic emotion disappears to be replaced by funereal lament.

[49] I do not accept the view that *elêxe*, "found its end," refers merely to a temporary cessation (see note on 956).

Polynices, the Chorus—almost in cold blood, if one can credit them with this—notes that in the case of "men of substance," jettisoning may bring safety; they immediately refer to Oedipus, who saved his city but was himself ruined. This sounds like a subtle comment on present possibilities: the ship of state may survive if some of its valuable cargo is jettisoned. This interpretation would fit in with the cryptic warning of Apollo (748–49); when the descendants are gone, the city is safe. It implies, of course, what I have asserted earlier, that there are no sisters.[50]

What we are left with is a hybrid text: 861–74, which introduce Antigone and Ismene, are interpolated, as are 1005–53 (the Herald and Antigone). As far as the "story" told by Aeschylus is concerned, 875–960 form a satisfactory ending. Further ritualistic lament and a processional exit would be appropriate (cf. *The Persians* and *The Eumenides*); the Chorus could divide to offer funeral processions to both brothers because the *Daimôn,* the evil destiny of the house, had ended all disagreements. Lines 961–1004 and 1054–78 may incorporate this ritualistic conclusion. They are of dubious authenticity; but I must admit that much of what is in the conclusion seems thoroughly Aeschylean in tone and that it sincerely develops the imagery of the preceding scenes. The felicity of the final picture, in particular (1075–78), leads me to agree that while the last fifth of the play disturbs the overall symmetry and harmony, the motives used here conform perfectly with those that form the pattern of the play. Few spurious passages can claim so authentic a tone.

Whatever the name of the play may have been, the subject is not the Seven who attacked Cadmeia but essentially Eteocles: a careful rational defender of his state against its foreign enemies, against panic-stricken citizens within, against seven enemy champions, and, in particular, against his own brother—a situation that resulted from chance, the draw of the lot nullifying all his careful planning, and that brought him face to face with that greater enemy, the evil destiny of his family

[50] A statement of the Chorus in 1054–56—a passage from an area of questionable authenticity (although I question it with considerable regret) —reflects the view that Eteocles and Polynices are the last of their line. Eteocles prayed that his city should not be uprooted *prumnothen panôlethron,* "root and branch in utter destruction" (71–72); the brothers were described as perishing *panôlethroi,* "in utter destruction" (933); now the Chorus adds that the family has been destroyed *prumnothen,* "root and branch" (1056). The association and ultimate separation of the city and the family of Laius are made absolutely clear, particularly by the emphatic placing of the word *houtôs,* "thus" (end of sentence, end of line 1056), implying, "The family was destroyed root and branch *as you see here.*"

and its efficient powers of vengeance. Every curtain Eteocles may have raised between himself and thoughts of his father's curse is now pulled away; all factors have conspired to concentrate attention on this one figure and his brother. It is no longer the Argives or the Seven, no longer brutes like Tydeus, but one man—his personal foe; it is no longer Mother Earth, Cadmeians, and Argives, but a specific mother, a specific father, and specific sons, all subject to the hatred of Apollo and to a disastrous family destiny.[51] A thinking man faces an incalculable superior power; his reaction is no willing sacrifice for the city, no hopeless surrender to supernatural powers; knowing full well what lies ahead he remains firmly and heroically at his post. The writer of the end of the play pays him a well-deserved, well-phrased compliment (1075–78). Especially effective in their splendid economy of language are the last two words, *ta malista*, "most of all," applicable both to the captain and the ship: *more than any other* he saved the ship of state from *utter* disaster.

APPENDIX A

Two brief accounts of the Oedipus story are of some relevance.

In *The Odyssey* 11. 271–80, Odysseus says that in the Underworld he saw Epicaste, who had married her own son, Oedipus, in ignorance; the marriage came after Oedipus had killed his own father—presumably in similar ignorance; later, however, the gods suddenly revealed the truth. Meanwhile Oedipus ruled at Thebes, where, for all the city's attractions, he suffered many troubles, thanks to the gods. Epicaste hanged herself and left Oedipus even more troubles, such as a mother's Furies create.

Aristophanes, *The Frogs* 1182–95, shows Aeschylus making fun of Euripides' prologues. He points out that Oedipus could never have been a fortunate man, as Euripides asserted, since, even before he was born, Apollo prophesied that he would kill his father; that he was exposed in an earthenware jar in winter time, so that he might not when *ektrapheis*, "grown up," kill his father; that he limped off with swollen feet to Polybus' house; that then, young as he was, he married an old woman —who proved to be his own mother! And so he blinded himself.

What is described in *The Frogs* is obviously a Euripidean develop-

[51] I am indebted for confirmation of the view that dramatic interest becomes concentrated on Eteocles to an unpublished paper by Mrs. Thomas Barry (Sharon Hirtle) of Yale University, which demonstrates the gradual limitation of words like "mother," "father," and "child" to the family of Oedipus in the second half of the play.

ment, and Aristophanes' criticism, put into the mouth of Aeschylus, seems to contain some shrewd points: exposure in winter sounds like a pathetic Euripidean touch; the use of the word *ektrapheis,* "grown up," ironically recalls the debt due to parents so much stressed in *The Seven Against Thebes* and probably developed by Euripides; as for *The Frogs* 1193, *graun egêmen autos ôn neos,* "and old woman he married though he himself was young," this is a double-barreled shot—it recalls Aeschylus' own metaphorical, less explicit comments on old sorrows mingled with new ones, but it is at the same time worthy of the Euripides who poked fun at the details of the recognition scene in Aeschylus' *The Libation Bearers.*

Aeschylus' version of the legend must lie, I think, between the simplicity of the Homeric statement and Euripidean detail.[52]

APPENDIX B

Creon, who is so important in the Theban plays of Sophocles, is merely mentioned here as father of one of the seven defenders, Megareus (474); the fact that a civic council replaced the dead Eteocles (1006), even if the passage is spurious, suggests that Aeschylus did not present him at any time as a probable regent. Tiresias, also prominent in Sophocles' plays, is referred to but is not brought on stage or even named; he is merely the blind prophet who warns of the imminent assault; he may, of course, have played an important part earlier as adviser to Oedipus and the queen. Oedipus' mother-wife is not named either; this may be due to the fact that she is here so closely linked with the whole concept of motherland and fatherland that had been violated as to be a symbol rather than a specific individual. No reference to any daughters of Oedipus is to be found in the first 860 lines of the play; any subsequent reference, direct or indirect, is probably due to an interpolator.[53]

---

[52] In *Olympian* 2. 38–46, Pindar notes that Theron, tyrant of Acragas, traced his ancestry back to Thersander, son of Polynices; he speaks of Oedipus' fateful killing of his father, Laius, and the Fury-inspired mutual destruction of Polynices and Eteocles; but for obvious diplomatic reasons he makes no mention of the incestuous marriage of Oedipus and his mother.

[53] For discussion of this problem, see pages 23–25.

CHARACTERS

CHORUS, *young Cadmeian women*

ETEOCLES, *son of Oedipus and present ruler of Thebes*

MESSENGER

SCOUT

[ANTIGONE } *sisters of* ETEOCLES
ISMENE

HERALD]

THE SEVEN AGAINST THEBES

Scene: The acropolis of the city. There are several altars and statues of gods at the edge of the orchestra. ETEOCLES enters.

ETEOCLES *Cadmeian citizens, right decisions*

---

1 In the preserved text the structure of the play is as follows:

1. Prologue: 1–77.
2. Entrance song of the CHORUS: 78–181.
3. First episode: 182–286.
4. First choral song: 287–368.
5. Second episode: 369–719.
6. Second choral song: 720–91.
7. Third episode: 792–821.
8. Third choral song: 822–1004.
9. Exit scene: 1005–78.

Rose very sensibly asks, "Whom does the actor address . . . ?" and adds, "I know no evidence that a choregus was put to such expense for *parachorêgêmata* [silent extras] as this would involve." He suggests that ETEOCLES addresses the audience as representing the citizens of his city. The prince refers (10–13) to three groups—the young, the old, and those of military age—but we must assume that the last group is absent on military duty.

must come from a city's captain, ready
for action, steering with unsleeping eyes.
Should all go well, the credit goes to god;

Cadmeian citizens: these words and *Cadmus' city* (9), which neatly frame the introductory passage, show ETEOCLES' real and immediate interest, his devotion to the city of his fathers. The Greek word *polis* and its derivative used here, *polîtai* (citizens), refer to a community whose members share common privileges and responsibility. What ETEOCLES implies here is something like, "Fellow citizens, we are in the same boat!"

right decisions must come: literally, it is necessary to utter *kairia* (things appropriate to a *kairos*, i.e., a critical moment or opportunity). This statement foreshadows ETEOCLES' apt comments on the first six attackers and their shields; ironically, it aligns him with Apollo, "a god who keeps quiet or speaks to the point" (619) and emphasizes his wish that the CHORUS would keep quiet (232, 250, 252, 262). He prides himself on his own ability to make appropriate decisions—an ability that leads to his own destruction and here, as elsewhere, contrasts human capacity with something called god (cf. note on 4). ETEOCLES begins with a calm appeal for loyal support by his fellow citizens. There may be a touch of petulance in his reference to god and the divided responsibility for human action. Perhaps he had been subjected to criticism because of the length of the siege.

2 *city's captain:* the recurrent nautical metaphor introduced here is discussed in the Introduction (pages 18–19). As implied above, ETEOCLES regards the citizens as a crew that ought to cooperate. The Greek says that the captain is at the stern, because this is where the steering-gear was; we should say "on the bridge." The helmsman-captain (*kubernêtês*) of a ship was an important figure; but as Plato indicates in *Republic* 6. 488 D-E, the abilities of a reasoning man were not always appreciated.

4 *The credit . . . god:* here and elsewhere (e.g., 21, 35, 625, 719) "god" or "gods" for ETEOCLES personally means little more than "luck," "chance" (see Introduction, pages 4–7 and cf. 550 and note). In any case he generally adopts an attitude like "Heaven helps those who help themselves!" and naturally has no sympathy with the hysterical CHORUS.

but if—god forbid!—disaster should strike, 5
one name alone, "Eteocles," would fill
the town, with citizens' loud-swelling chants
of lament. From this may Zeus Protector,
true to his name, protect Cadmus' city!
And now, your task. You that fall short of ripe 10

---

5 *god forbid:* little more than a conventional formula (literally, may it not happen).

6 *one name . . . fill:* the Greek here juxtaposes two words *heis polus* (single much, or one many) and bythis juxtaposition intensifies the value of each word. The introduction of the name of ETEOCLES in this line is a characteristic piece of exposition.

7 *loud-swelling chants:* the Greek here is, literally, something like "would be hymned in much-surging preludes that are laments." ETEOCLES takes phraseology that would normally refer to hymns of triumph or preludes praising the gods and turns it inside out. An extended use of this technique of inversion will be found in lines 854–60. Here the somewhat quizzical attitude of ETEOCLES toward the gods is neatly displayed. "Loud-swelling" involves the word *rhothos,* which implies a splashing noise like that of oars, for instance; the word occurs in other compound forms *takhurrothous* (flurry of foaming), 285; *epirrothon* (one wave . . . another), 368. A verbal form is used in Sophocles, *Antigone* 259, where accusations were hurled noisily back and forth by the guards. The word fits the general nautical imagery; this is one of the tides ETEOCLES has to cope with.

8 *of lament:* Aeschylus has used a metaphorical expression and immediately explains it.

9 *true to his name:* the magic ritual of invocation demanded that a deity be addressed by the right name to evoke his power effectively; this can be seen throughout Greek literature, even in the famous mock-appeal of Sappho to Aphrodite, the "weaver of trickery." At the same time we must recognize the incorrigible Greek love of word-play; above all, names must mean something.

10 *And . . . task:* ETEOCLES has stated his own position; the crew's duty comes next; they are to act while he makes the right decisions. The situation is given in three stages, all marked by the word *nûn,* "now" (*and now,* 10, the general picture; *well, until today,* 21, the situation brought up to date; *but now,* 24, the specific situation).

maturity, you that are past the prime,
cherishing to the full your body's growth,
and those in life's prime season, as befits them,
must guard the town, the altars of its native gods,
to keep their honor unimpaired, protect 15
the children and the motherland, a nurse
most dear, who, welcoming all nurture's toil,
upon her kindly bosom reared creeping
young shoots, to settle homes and bear a shield
in loyal repayment at this her time of need. 20
Well, until today we have had good luck;
through all the time we have been under siege
most of the fight has gone well, thanks to god.

---

12 *cherishing* (*aldainein*): a word appropriate to plant growth; it is used in 557, where Actor will not allow evil weeds to grow.

12–13 I do not reverse the order of 12 and 13 as Murray does in OCT[2].

14 The word order is significant: first city, then gods.

16–20 See Introduction, pages 19–22, for general comment on this passage. It is a comprehensive picture: the creeping young shoots are to grow up to be householders and loyal shield-bearers; they will owe this duty of defense to the parents and land that reared them. Reference to shield-bearers foreshadows the shield descriptions in the middle of the play, and "loyal repayment," as indicated earlier on page 20, reflects one of the basic features of the story.

17 *welcoming . . . toil:* a word used here *pandokousa* (all-welcoming), which in later Greek refers to somebody like an innkeeper, is recalled in line 860 (*pandokon*), where it is applied most appropriately to the world of the dead—no doubt, the land that welcomed back its own. At the same time, we are reminded that in the Oedipus story not all parents welcomed the upbringing of their children.

20 The last Greek word in this sentence is *tode* (this). Its position—end of sentence, end of line—is important: of all crises, *this* is the one—*right here and now.*

21–23 These lines indicate that the siege has gone on for some time—not surprisingly; the Greeks seem to have been somewhat inept in this form of warfare.

But now speaks our prophet, expert augur,
who notes, with ear and mind, without fire's help, 25
the birds of omen, with unerring skill;
he, ruler in his own realm, prophecy,
says that the strongest Achaean assault
is being plotted this night against our town.
So, to the battlements and city gates 30
speed all of you at once in full array;
man the bulwarks; on the turrets' gangways
take your place, and at the gateway exits
stand firm courageously; invading hordes
must not cause panic. God will give us luck! 35

---

24 *But now:* the third and specific *nûn.* Matters have come to a crisis as some seer—one well known, obviously, as the simple phrase "the seer" implies—has informed ETEOCLES. The seer is presumably Tiresias, but he is not named in the play (see Introduction, page 27). He is apparently blind: he does not prophesy by sacrificial fires or victims, but by what must be a peculiarly acute sensitivity to the flight and cries of birds. ETEOCLES credits him with unerring skill (26); he is a thinker like ETEOCLES himself (25); and the prince recognizes the seer as a fellow ruler—in his own special field (27). Even if he is sarcastic, ETEOCLES does pay enough heed to take the necessary precautions, although he clearly relies also on his own careful measures (36–38) and welcomes the SCOUT's confirming report.

27 The Greek of this line comes close to saying: "this man, ruler in this sort of thing, prophecy."

29 The night is just finishing and dawn beginning. Sophocles' *Antigone* also begins about dawn, but there the enemy has been routed during the night.

32 The sentence begins with the usual Greek word for manning a ship, and the words translated "bulwarks" and "gangways" are thus given nautical color.

35 If ETEOCLES and his men do their part, god will no doubt cooperate. The brief reference to god and luck is immediately followed by reference to practical measures. There is some of Sophocles' efficient Oedipus in ETEOCLES; he has attended to matters inside the city; he has also seen to outside intelligence.

For my part, scouts and spies on enemy moves—
I sent them; these, I know, will not waste time;
with their news no trickery will trip me.

The SCOUT enters.

SCOUT *Eteocles, Cadmeia's eminent prince,*
I bring you clear news from the battlefield— 40
clear, because I myself saw what went on.
Seven heroes, valiant company leaders,
slit a bull's throat over a black-rimmed shield
and, dipping their fingers in the bull's blood,
by Ares, Enyo, and bloodthirsty Fear 45
swore that they would either raze the city,
violently sacking the Cadmeian town,
or, dying, thickly blend this soil with blood.
Remembrance-gifts to their parents at home

---

38 There is considerable irony here in ETEOCLES' certainty that his careful planning and intelligence will bring success. (The SCOUT expresses the same kind of confidence in 67–68.) One may almost detect a kind of emphatic finality in the passage, since 37 and 38 end with pararhymes (*hodôi, dolôi*) in a fashion that recalls a Shakespearean scene ending.

40*ff* He can offer clear information, but not the names—which proves important when ETEOCLES, self-appointed seventh champion, finds that he himself must face his brother.

42 *valiant:* in Greek *thourios,* a Homeric word, in Homer applied only to Ares; in *The Persians* 73, 718, and 754 it is applied to Xerxes.

43*ff* What this obviously solemn ritual actually meant is not clear; apparently they bound themselves together by blood sacred to certain deities and swore a common oath, perhaps like people swearing on the Bible.

47 Part of this vow is repeated by Parthenopaeus in 531. See also 427 (Capaneus).

48 On this mixture of blood and soil, see Introduction, pages 20–22.

49 Ironically, of the seven offerings (buckles, locks of hair, scarfs, according to the lexicographer Hesychius) only one may have reached home, that of Polynices, since Adrastus had to abandon his chariot

they draped on Adrastus' chariot, weeping— 50
but no cry of self-pity left their lips.
For a steely will with flaming courage
stirred them, like lions with fight in their eyes.
No man's delay holds back proof of my news.
For they were casting lots when I left, to learn 55
which gate each must attack with his forces.
And so, our finest men, the city's choice,
must be marshalled at the gates—and at once.
You know, by now the full Argive force is near,

---

and flee on his divine horse, Arion. Adrastus, king of Argos, father-in-law of Polynices and Tydeus, was leader of the expedition. It is typical of the word-play so common in Greek literature that his name should suggest "one not likely to run away."

52–53 *steely will, flaming courage, like lions:* metaphorical concepts that are developed in the description of the attackers later.

54 There are two possible Greek readings here: *pistis* (confirmation), and *pustis* (information); the general effect is much the same. Either the attackers were so nearly ready to move that they would soon bring proof of the SCOUT's report or the SCOUT lost no time in bringing the news because the attackers were right on his heels.

55–56 The positions of the Argive attackers were the result of chance, of the lot, as is mentioned several times later; ETEOCLES meets this process by judicious selection, to bring about his own disaster.

57–58 This is what ETEOCLES is busy doing off-stage in 78–181. Two details may be noted: the SCOUT ends his sentence *tâgeusai takhos* (do your marshalling quickly); the sound pattern emphasizes the urgency; but the verbal form used (the Greek "middle" voice) implies that ETEOCLES will direct arrangements, get men stationed, rather than participate in person.

59ff The Argive force that raises the dust is likened to a stormy sea that threatens the city; the metaphor is developed fully and includes a fairly common play on the Argive name, which suggests *argos* (shining, white), and lines 59 and 60 end respectively *Argeiôn stratos* (Argive force) and *argistês aphros* (whitening foam). The pictorial association of whitening foam with horses is natural, since Poseidon, the sea-god, is also god of horses (see 130).

on the march, raising the dust; and whitening foam 60
flecks the ground with froth from the horses' snorting.
So, like a skilled ship's captain, barricade
the city, before the squalls of Ares
sweep down; loudly roars this land-surge of men.
And here you must decide with the greatest speed. 65
Next, I shall keep as faithful watch by day
as by night; informed by my clear account
of enemy moves, you will stay unharmed.

The SCOUT leaves.

ETEOCLES *O Zeus, Earth, and gods that guard our city,*

---

62 *like . . . captain:* the phrase was or became apparently proverbial; it was used by Euripides, *Medea* 523, perhaps humorously, when Jason answers Medea's torrent of words: "Well, I'll have to be a skilled ship's captain to weather this storm."

63 *squalls of Ares:* this detail recurs in the CHORUS' expansion of the sea-storm image (115).

64 *land-surge:* Aeschylus seems to feel it necessary to qualify his metaphor; the army is a *kûma khersaion* (a wave on land). Similar qualifications are *ardis apuros* (an arrow point not forged with fire, the gadfly's sting, *Prometheus Bound* 880); *akrageis kunas* (dogs, which do not bark, eagles, *Prometheus Bound* 803); *pedais akhalkeutais* (fetters not made of bronze, the robe which entangled Agamemnon, *The Libation Bearers* 493).

65 The SCOUT speaks ETEOCLES' language: ETEOCLES spoke about making opportune decisions; the SCOUT urges him to seize the opportunity.

66 Another indication of time: the SCOUT has been out by night; he will now go by daylight.

67–68 Again he speaks ETEOCLES' language; but, like ETEOCLES in 38, he is mistaken.

69*ff* ETEOCLES is left alone and permits himself a brief cry of anguish. He naturally makes an appeal to the city's gods; then, though apparently fully in command of the situation, gives a momentary glimpse of his personal concern. But immediately he returns to anxiety for his city. One detail is worthy of notice: ETEOCLES says *mê moi polin ge*, where the particle *ge* is important; like the Latin

my father's curse, mighty vengeful Spirit, 70
do not blot out my city, root and branch,
utterly destroyed by enemies' hands,
a Greek city, with its established homes.
The land is free; so is Cadmus' city;
never let slavery's yoke subdue them. 75
Be our defense. My hopes concern you, too;

---

quidem it usually stresses or underlines what precedes, so that ETEOCLES says, "Do not, I pray you, (wipe out) my *city* at least"; he says nothing about himself, but he does dwell on his city's merits.

70 This is the only mention of the curse (see Introduction, pages 16–18) in this play until the shocked outcry of 655. But we must remember that the utterance of the curse must have come, probably fairly late, in the preceding play; that, in turn, must have recalled the *Erinys* or Fury brought on the family by Laius' disobedience. This brief reference would tend to keep the audience alert for subsequent developments. For the present, however, the city's danger overshadows the threat of the curse.

71–72 *blot out . . . root and branch:* in Greek, *ekthamnisête . . . prumnothen.* The first word means literally "extirpate"; and since the second suggests *prumna*, the stern of a ship, Rose feels that we have a mixed metaphor here. I doubt this; but I do feel that Aeschylus made an almost mischievous use of a word which means "from the bottom" or "root" (by some lexicographers spelled *premnothen*) and thus recalled the word *prumnêthen* (from the stern)—thereby recalling both of the basic metaphors. In any case the phrase "root and branch" along with "utterly destroyed" (72) becomes peculiarly applicable to ETEOCLES' family (see Introduction, pages 23–25).

73*ff* See Introduction, footnote 31.

74–75 The sentence and 74 begin with the word "free"; 75 begins with "slavery's yoke"; a good actor could easily make this metrical emphasis significant.

76–77 This bargaining aspect of divine worship is one which might well interest the somewhat skeptical ETEOCLES. It is exploited considerably in Aristophanes' *The Birds;* but we should here note more serious comments like those of the CHORUS in 177–80, 304–20, and

a city that fares well honors its gods.

ETEOCLES leaves to arrange for defense of the city. The CHORUS enters in great excitement, perhaps in ones and twos; the first utterances may be sung by single voices rather than in unison.

CHORUS *I shriek in fear of dreadful sufferings.*

---

716 (or of Orestes in *The Libation Bearers* 255–63). ETEOCLES' pragmatic, *quid pro quo* attitude is clearly shown in lines 217–18.

78–181 *Parodos* (entrance song of the CHORUS). The first section (78–108) is divided by Murray in his OCT[2] into eleven separate utterances. After this excited beginning the CHORUS is gradually brought to order by the CHORUS LEADER, who apparently addresses them in 100 and 103; after an excited appeal to Ares, they move up to the statues of the deities worshiped locally and call on them in general and separately. Their prayers are interrupted and spurred on by real or imagined noises; but the ode ends with two moderately calm stanzas (166–72, 173–81) addressed to the gods in general. "For an early play, the parodos of the CHORUS is bold and novel; they do not march on to a system of anapests, as in the *Suppl.* and *Persae*" says H. J. Rose in his *Commentary*, I. 169. The descriptive part of his statement is true; the passage is unexampled in extant Greek drama for excitement. But the implied comparison is a dangerous one: first, this is not very early in the history of Greek drama; second, it is now clear that *The Suppliants* is not an early and primitive play of Aeschylus, but later than *The Seven Against Thebes* (see Lesky, pages 58–60); but above all, we should remember that apart from *The Persians*, the anapestic *parodoi* occur in the first plays of trilogies, *The Suppliants* and *Agamemnon*; the first choral utterances in *The Libation Bearers* and *The Eumenides* are by no means anapestic; and in *Prometheus Bound*, probably the first play in a late trilogy, the anapests are arrogated by Prometheus. Whatever the pattern may have been, dramatic considerations alone explain this "novel" entrance song.

The metres used by the CHORUS are dochmiacs and lyric iambs. There are two basic forms of dochmiacs: ⏑ – – ⏑ – and – ⏑ ⏑ – ⏑ –; each of these may have its long syllables resolved into two short syllables, and there are many similar combinations, which are classified by scholars under the general heading of dochmiacs. (Cf. the five long syllables of 116: *all' o Zeu, pheu pheu.*) By lyric iambs

I refer to free combinations of iambic metra (⏓–⏑–) and approximate equivalents (the cretic –⏑– or bacchius ⏑––), as in 119, for instance (*pantôs arêxon dáïôn halôsin* –––⏑/––⏑–/⏑––), or 123 (*kinûrontai phonon khalînoi* ⏑––/–⏑–/⏑–––). The dochmiac metre especially lends itself to excited utterance. After their first cry of distress (78) the Chorus vividly portrays the rush of the enemy flood from behind its barriers as follows:

mĕthēitāi strătōs   strătŏpĕdōn lĭpōn
rhēi pŏlŭs hŏdē lĕōs   prŏdrŏmŏs hīppŏtās

where the plain opening dochmiac is followed by a group of resolved dochmiacs, the rhythm, like the army, set free from constraint. An instructive resolved onomatopoeic dochmiac is found in 86: *hudatos orotupou* (water that strikes on a mountain) refers to a mountain torrent.

Excited rhythms and difficulties in the text have caused dissension among editors about the structure of the parados. There can be no doubt that 78–108 are freely astrophic and that 166–81 form a strophe and antistrophe. The lines between these passages have been arranged in my translation, as in Murray's OCT² into two strophe-antistrophe pairs (109–49, 150–65). Whatever the detailed pattern may be, one can see a general development from free, excited rhythms to ones more regulated, though still excited.

It should be noted that the young women must have heard the Scout's news (see 124–27) and, presumably, the augur's warning that a desperate effort is about to be made by the enemy to end the lengthy siege. This has alarmed them, and their fears are increased by the noises, real or imagined, of the approaching forces. It is not too difficult to accept their fears of the preliminary bombardment (158), but why they should be so tremendously impressed by the enemy's horses and chariots, although dramatically effective, is not reasonably explained. The behavior of the Chorus comes in sharp contrast to the statesman-like, rational attitude of Eteocles, and the contrast is intensified by the Chorus' exploitation of the image with which the play begins; they develop to the full the picture of the heavy seas and storms that the ship of state's captain has to fear.

78 Literally translated: "I utter fearful great sufferings." The Chorus leaves no doubt about what they propose to do; they almost give their entrance song a title.

Their army is let loose, it has left the camp.
A mighty flood of men is out there, cavalry rushing ahead. 80
The dust rising in the air persuades me—I see it,
a wordless, yet clear and effective messenger.
Hard on the surface of our land has fallen the clash of horses' hoofs!
Listen! the uproar comes closer.
It surges aloft and booms, 85
relentless like the crashing of a mountain torrent.
O gods and goddesses, now that it is stirred up,
fend off disaster!
Out beyond our walls 90

---

79 The language suggests the opening of a barrier that has been holding back water; but the confusion of the rush of horses with the rush of a torrent does not exclude possible connotations of the start of a horse race.

80 Clearly shows the confusion just noted. The cavalry naturally outdistances the foot-soldiers.

81–82 The CHORUS now gets visible evidence of the report it has heard. The same metaphor is found in *Suppl.* 188 ("I see dust, the voiceless messenger of an army"), and in Theognis 549 a beacon is called a "voiceless messenger."

83–90 The text here is uncertain. At 84 and 86, Murray in OCT² resorts to transcribing the word *boâi* as a stage direction (shouts off); one wonders who raised the shout. I offer the sense of what can be called at best a reasonable composite text.

83ff The visual evidence is replaced by noise, and again the rush of horses is spoken of in terms of rushing waters; but the mixture of pictures persists in "it surges aloft." Much of this ode has onomatopoeic value, derived both from the freely resolved dochmiacs and from the actual sounds: here the rhythm of the heavy line 85 is followed by a speedy rattling dochmiac—*potâtai, bremei d'/ amakhetou dikân hudatos orotupou* (it flies, it roars like irresistible water that strikes a mountain). The noise arouses excited appeal to the gods; the threat of the enemy—now, they feel, close to the walls—leads to momentary despair. But the CHORUS pulls itself together, stops its shrieking, and proceeds to more rational appeal to the chief Cadmeian gods.

that host with silver-bright shields presses on, well set
to attack our city, rapidly advancing.
Who now will rescue us, who have power to save,
whether god or goddess?
At the feet of the statues, then, shall I kneel, 95
before our country's gods?
Yes, you that sit in blessedness,
it is high time to grasp your statues. Why do we
wait and wail in dismay?

CHORUS LEADER *Do you hear or not the clatter of shields?* 100

CHORUS *Sacred robes and wreaths—when if not now shall we place them in prayer on the statues?*

---

91 *silver-bright shields:* there is probably here a veiled pun in the adjective *leukaspis* (white-shielded) similar to that commented on above (59); the pun is made specific in Sophocles, *Antigone* 106 (the white-shielded man from Argos) and Euripides, *The Phoenician Women* 1106 (the white-shielded host of Argos).

95*ff* Here the CHORUS, probably urged on by the CHORUS LEADER (100, 103), moves toward the statues of the local gods. It is consistent with Aeschylus' portrayal of the city attacked as the city of Cadmus rather than the historic Thebes that he does not include Dionysus and Heracles among the "native gods" in this play. Cf. also 528, where there is no indication that Amphion built the walls of Thebes (as in Euripides, *The Phoenician Women* 114–16). The deities are enumerated in the following lines: Ares (104, 135), Zeus (116), Pallas Athena (129, 161), Poseidon (131), Cypris (140), Apollo (145, 159), Artemis (147, 154), Hera (151), Pallas Onca (163). Some of them have especially close links with the city: Ares and Cypris (see notes on 104, 105, 135, 140) and Onca (see note on 164).

98 *high time:* like ETEOCLES they feel that this is a crisis; but their reaction is different.

100 See 103 below.

101–102 The ceremony of adorning statues with garments and flowers goes back to the epic times at least (*The Iliad* 6. 87ff and 271ff). Verrall suggested that the robes and wreaths were already decorating the statues, since the fugitives would bring no offerings.

CHORUS LEADER *See! a clash: that clatter means many shields!*

CHORUS *What will you do, Ares, who have dwelt so long in this land?*
Will you betray your own? 105
God of the golden helmet, look, look on this city
which once you cherished and loved!

---

103 This line and 100 were probably spoken by the CHORUS LEADER; the meter is regular iambic trimeter in contrast with the dochmiacs of the CHORUS. Emphasis on clattering shields stresses the need for litany. In 103 I retain the reading of the manuscripts and the scholiast (*dedorka*, "I see", rather than *dedoika*, "I fear", of the OCT[2]) as a splendid example of synaesthesis, by no means alien to Aeschylus, in spite of Murray's *vix credibile;* the CHORUS "pictures" the noise.

The sound of these lines is worthy of note; *akouet' ê ouk akouet' aspidôn ktupon* (100) and *ktupon dedorka; patagon oukh henos doros* (103). *Patagon* is a good onomatopoeic word, used elsewhere for the chattering of a coward's teeth or the splatter of hail on the sea.

104ff After alarmed description of what is happening around the city as they hear it or see it, but chiefly imagine it, in auditory and visual terms, the CHORUS ends the first part of the entrance song with an appeal to Ares, who is responsible for what is frightening them, although at the same time he is partly responsible for the origin of the Cadmeian people (see next note). Because of his relationship to Cadmus, as father of Harmonia, one might expect him to be a helped, not an attacker. But also Ares might feel anger at the killing of the serpent that guarded his spring. Ares was in an equivocal position; so, in 115, for example, one could regard Ares as an abstraction, not a pertinent mythological, genealogical figure. In some ways Ares is just as incalculable as other forces that ETEOCLES has to face.

105 *your own:* the land was Ares' because (a) the serpent from whose teeth the Sown Men grew was his ward (Euripides, *The Phoenician Women* 931–35) and (b) Cadmus' wife Harmonia was the daughter of Ares and Aphrodite.

STROPHE 1

Gods that guard our city and country, come, all of you,
come, look on us, mere girls, 110
a company praying to escape slavery!
Pouring around the city are men with wind-swept crests,
a seething surge stirred up by Ares' blasts. 115
Come, O Zeus, come Father all-powerful,

---

109 The first excited nonstrophic lyrics of the CHORUS end here. What follows varies between fairly rational appeals to the gods and frequent excited interjections. After a prayer to the civic gods in general (109ff), justified by the threats so vividly described, the CHORUS turns to Zeus and once more stresses the immediate threat to the city (116–27); what may be an antistrophe (128–49) addresses three pairs of deities: Pallas and Poseidon, whose important connection with Athens might exert some influence on the emotions of the audience; Ares and Aphrodite, associated with the beginnings of the Cadmeian city, and appropriately given six lines in the middle of the stanza; Apollo and Artemis. The noise of chariots and a shower of spears evoke appeals to Hera and Artemis (150–57); slingshots and the clatter of arms evoke appeals to Apollo, presumably Athena, and finally Onca, the goddess before the gates (158–65). As the CHORUS appeals to each of the gods we may assume that some kind of choreographic movement would allow them to pass from statue to statue during the song. The final strophe (166–73) and antistrophe (174–81) again call on the gods in general, bidding them respect and remember the worship the CHORUS and the city have paid them.

110–111 *mere girls, a company:* they are unmarried, but of marriageable age; and this has considerable effect in their subsequent picture of what a city's capture means to people like themselves and to women of other ages and positions in life. The word *lokhon* (company) is the same as that used in line 56, there translated "forces"; the group ETEOCLES has to cope with inside the city is similar to the enemy outside. See also 194.

114–115 The now familiar picture is intensified by the addition of whitecaps, the tossing plumes.

at all costs ward off capture by the foe.
The Argives now hold Cadmus' city 120
encircled; and we fear the enemy's power.
From the jaws of the horses—you hear?—
comes a wail of bloodshed as the bits rattle.
And seven proud warriors, their army's best,
brandishing the spears they hold, 125
at each of the seven gates take
their stand as the lot assigned.

ANTISTROPHE 1

And you, daughter of Zeus that love battle,
Pallas, come as our savior!
And god of horses, lord that rule the sea 130
with a weapon that spears the fish, Poseidon,
deliver us from fear, grant deliverance!
And Ares, help the city with Cadmus' name, 135
give it protective care by visible act!

---

118 This line significantly reechoes Eteocles' emphasis on the safety of the city (71), but nobody as yet realizes what "at all costs" will mean.

120–121 An interesting sentence in Greek: *Aregeioi . . . polisma Kadmeiôn/kukloüntai*—"the Argives . . . the city of the Cadmeians/ are encircling," syntactically as well as in fact. The forces around the city are compared later to a coiled snake (290–91).

124ff This shows that the Scout's news had spread through the city.

130 Poseidon is said to have created the horse and to have taught men to bridle and tame it; Adrastus' divine horse, Arion, and Pegasus were his offspring. The combination of sea-god and horse-god is obviously valuable for the poet's imagery.

131 *weapon:* the trident (though some have thought it to be a harpoon).

135 For the association of Ares with the city and Cadmus, see Introduction, pages 19–20, and notes on 104 and 105. As in Homer, Ares might move among the soldiers and inspire them; so, success here might seem like an epiphany.

Cypris, too, as primal mother of our race, 140
defend us; you are the source that gave us
birth; with prayers god-directed
we cry out and come before you.
You, too, Lycian lord, prove true to your name, 145
devouring the enemy's forces!
And you, maiden daughter of Leto, make ready your bow!

STROPHE 2

Listen, listen!
The clatter of chariots—I hear them—round the city, 150
O lady Hera,
creaking from the sockets of heavily burdened axles!
Artemis beloved!
filled with whirring spears the air flutters madly. 155

---

140 *primal mother:* as mother of Harmonia, Cadmus' wife.

145 *Lycian lord:* the adjective with its various connotations cannot be translated adequately. It may be related to some cult in Lycia; it may be derived from *lukos* (wolf) because of a tradition that Apollo drove out wolves from some area; or it may be associated with Apollo as bringer of dawn (*lukê*). As Apollo Nomius, protector of herds, he might well be regarded as protector against wolves; but he might also be as destructive as a wolf—just as he could be both bringer and healer of disease. Aeschylus is undoubtedly playing especially on the second meaning; the CHORUS is saying, "Lycian lord, prove Lycian," i.e., "prove yourself a true Wolf-god." In Sophocles, *Electra* 6, the old servant tells Orestes, "Here is the market place called Lycian after the wolf-slaying god."

149 *Listen, listen:* an effort to represent a gasping cry (*e, e, e, e*) which like most Greek exclamations is untranslatable.

150–165 The CHORUS, roused by fresh noises, call as women first on Hera and Artemis; then, as citizens—mentioning Apollo perhaps almost automatically in association with Artemis or perhaps as guardian of the city streets—they appeal to Athena and the city goddess Onca.

What is our city's fate, what will become of it?
what is the outcome to which god leads?

ANTISTROPHE 2

Listen, listen!
From the slingers falls a shower of stones on our battlements,
beloved Apollo!
Clanging at the gates, clanging of bronze-bordered shields! 160
Child of Zeus, from whom comes
decision in battle, a sanctioned end to fighting,
and you, blessed lady, Onca, set before our city,
give your home of seven gates defense! 165

STROPHE 3

O deities of mighty power,
O gods and goddesses of accomplishment
that guard the bulwarks of our land,

156–157 Once more interest is concentrated on the city's welfare with no realization of what the outcome really will be. Meanwhile the audience waits to see how the outcome will be achieved.

158 Wilamawitz's emendation, adopted in Murray's text, seems to me unavoidable. Alternatives to the translation must mean: (a) the enemy's slingshots do not reach high enough to hit the defenders —this should cause no great alarm; or (b) the defenders hurl slingshots from the battlements—but the Chorus never seems to take into account that there are human defenders.

161–162 If, as is likely, this passage refers to Athena, she will resemble Athena Nike, goddess of victory.

164–165 Onca is often, but apparently not here, identified with Athena. Ancient sources suggest that she was a Phoenician deity, whose cult was established in Boeotia by Cadmus. Her shrine was actually at one of the gates, not inside the city.

166–180 Whatever their views on what precedes, scholars agree that here the parados (entrance song) offers a strophe and antistrophe (166–73, 174–81). With dramatic and musical effectiveness the Chorus calms down to a more rational and solemn appeal for help.

do not betray our city, center of strife,
to an enemy with an alien tongue. 170
Hear us, mere girls, hear our prayers as is right
while we lift up our hands before you.

ANTISTROPHE 3

O deities whom we cherish,
with deliverance surround and guard our city; 175
show clearly that you cherish it.
Bethink you of the city's sacred offerings,
and, as you think of them, bring rescue!
yes, and the city's loving rites of sacrifice— 180
be mindful of them, we pray you.

ETEOCLES enters in anger.

---

170 *enemy with an alien tongue:* see Introduction, note 31. In the immediate context I doubt that the phrase means anything more than "a fearful enemy."

171 *mere girls . . . as is right:* they, more than any others, they feel, deserve to be heard and pitied. See 110.

175 *surround:* in Greek, *amphibantes polin* (having taken a stand around the city). This is a picture that recalls the protective attitude of a Homeric hero who tries to protect a fallen comrade from being despoiled. It may have become a commonplace in appeals to deities: in *Iliad* 1. 37, the priest prays to Apollo, *hos Khrûsên amphibebêkas* (you that have taken your stand around [the city of] Chryse); and it is likely that a scrap of a hymn addressed by Alcaeus to a Boeotian Athena (Lobel-Page, Alcaeus Z 1; Diehl, frag. 3, used the same verb to describe her as a protecting deity.

177–180 A similar *quid pro quo* to that of ETEOCLES in 76–77, except that ETEOCLES speaks of prospective future rewards.

180 *yes, and:* a Greek particle here (*toi*) has a certain admonitory effect.

181 *we pray you:* the last word in this ode is *moi,* dative of the first personal pronoun—singular, it is true; but the CHORUS often refer to themselves as an individual group. Grammatically the word might be called an *ethic* dative and in older translations might

ETEOCLES *You insufferable creatures, I ask you,*
is this conduct best, does it help our town?

---

have been represented by *prithee.* Whatever terminology one chooses to apply, this word placed last in a choral ode of more than 100 lines must be important; the poet could have put it anywhere else if he had wanted to do so.

A *general note on the entrance song:*

The Greek language seems to have a large complement of *p-* and *t-* sounds, but assonance and consonance based on these sounds together with effective rhythms and verbal echoes make this ode noteworthy. I have already suggested some of these features in the commentary: for instance, the excitement that follows the CHORUS' first slow dissyllable *threumai* (78ff); the heavy beginning of 116 (*all' ô Zeu pheu pheu*) followed by *pater panteles pantôs,* an emphatic alliterative appeal; there are clattering words like *patagos* (clatter, 103) or *konabos* (clanging, 160) and characteristic, almost ritualistic, repetitions like *kluete parthenôn, kluete pandikôs* (hear us, mere girls, hear . . . . as is right, 171) add solemnity to the sound effects.

182–286 *First episode.* ETEOCLES' reentry is an angry one: he has been interrupted while trying to arrange defenses for these very people who are hindering his efforts by their demoralizing panic. It is probably particularly galling to ETEOCLES that they do nothing constructive (see 183) and merely rely frantically on the gods. Instead of contributing *tharsos* (bold courage) 184, women are likely to be themselves embodiments of boldness, not courage, bold creatures like the Helen of *Agamemnon* 803, or terrified hindrances, as in this case (191–94). Lines 194–95 have terrible implications in the light of ETEOCLES' own family history; indeed, it may well be that thoughts of his mother, mother-wife of Oedipus, may have so influenced him as to encourage this tirade. (In fact, ETEOCLES' utterances here help to confirm my feeling that there were no sisters in Aeschylus' play. See Introduction, pages 24–25.) After his mixture of generalizations and specific references, ETEOCLES lays down the penalty for disobedience and ends with a picture of woman's proper place—at least in a wartime society.

creatures: the Greek *thremmata* (things nourished) clearly reflects the mother-growth image; the adjective "unbearable" offers many connotations.

183 *best:* I retain the manuscript's *arista* (best), for which Murray

encourage the forces here under siege?
flinging yourselves on the city-gods' statues, 185
yelling, shrieking—utter absurdities!
Never in bad luck or—better—in good,
may I have to share life with womankind!
Successful, she's haughty, not fit to live with;
scared, she hurts her home, even more her town. 190
So, in our townsfolk these foaming rushes
you started have spread cowardly dismay.

---

reads in OCT[2]—incorrectly—*arôga* (helpful). ETEOCLES is using specific parliamentary language; the word is found frequently in Attic decrees. Characteristically his first thought is for the city.

184 *encourage:* the Greek word used here is *tharsos;* see 189 with note.

186 *yelling:* the Greek word is onomatopoeic, *auein,* suggesting the howling of a dog.

utter absurdities: literally, "things hated by sensible people." The phrase is best taken as a vocative, addressed to the women; but it could be taken in apposition with "yelling, shrieking," a philosophical comment less likely from ETEOCLES, whose attitude is further expressed in 188, where he says *gunaikeiôi genei* (woman's category, anything female). Presumably he considers himself one of the "sensible people" and here, in that capacity, tries to calm the women. The word *genos* (race, class), used here in the dative, *genei,* is not necessarily derogatory: for instance, Hesiod, *Theogony* 346, speaks of a *hieron* (sacred) *genos* of daughters born by Thetis; *genos* is justified by the fact that there are 41 of them, and the adjective "sacred" makes their nature clear. More striking however is Hesiod's statement in *Theogony* 590–92: "[From her (*sc.* Pandora) comes the class of females;] from her come the destructive class and groups of women, who are a mighty plague as they live among mortal men."

188 ETEOCLES had some knowledge of what it meant: Laius with his wife; that wife with her own son, Oedipus.

189 *haughty:* the Greek uses *thrasos,* a variant form of *tharsos* (courage, 184), at times implying something derogatory.

190 Naturally he mentions a woman's home first, but more emphasis is given to the community.

191 *foaming rushes:* the women resemble, even cooperate with, the stormy waves of men outside.

Thus, the enemy's cause is well advanced
while we are ruined from within by our own.
That's what one can get, living with women! 195
So, if any refuse to heed my words,
man or woman, any creature at all,
a vote of death shall be cast against him,
public stoning—a fate he can't escape.
It's men's job—no place for women's plans here!— 200
what lies outside. Stay home, and cause no trouble!
Do you hear or not? or do I find you deaf?

STROPHE 1

CHORUS *Oedipus' dear son, I was scared when I heard*

194–195 Connotations of this line have already been noted on 182–286. But it may be well to refer to lines 200–202 and 230–32, where ETEOCLES distinguishes those who are to deal with matters outside from those who are concerned with matters inside. By following his own precepts he ends what is definitely an "inside" matter, his own family's fate.

197 ETEOCLES actually says "anything that lies between." The phrase has no specific connotations; he is just too angry to speak with complete coherence.

198–199 Literally, "a voting pebble for destruction will be deliberated"—a play on the word *psêphos*, a pebble for voting; the word-play is clarified in 199: "fate by stoning." Technically, of course, such references to voting and deliberation are anachronistic. Herodotus tells how a certain Lycidas, a member of the Athenian *boulê* (a deliberative body or senate), was stoned to death for proposing that Athens accept the peace terms offered by the Persian Mardonius; when word of this reached the Athenian women, evacuated to Salamis, they stoned to death Lycidas' wife and children. There may well have been memories of such a lynching in 479 B.C. that would recur in the minds of an Athenian audience twelve years later. At any rate the story became an ingredient in the patriotic utterances of Athenians; the story is referred to by Demosthenes and Lycurgus in the fourth century B.C.

200 A fairly common view first expressed by Hector in *Iliad* 6. 492. Here, see also 230–32 and 262; perhaps 194–95.

202 The CHORUS is certainly not deaf, but they hear the wrong things.

203– After ETEOCLES' angry criticism of the CHORUS, he engages in an

the clattering, rattling din of the chariots
and the shrill screeching of the whirling axle-naves, 205
when the horses' guiding-gear clanged in their mouths,
the fire-wrought bits that steer them.

ETEOCLES *Tell me, can any sailor by rushing*
from stern to prow find a way of safety
for his ship, hard pressed in mid-ocean's waves? 210

ANTISTROPHE 1

CHORUS *No, it is to the gods I came in my rush,*
these old statues, trusting heaven, when the baleful

---

244 interchange with the CHORUS or the CHORUS LEADER. Six lyric stanzas (dochmiacs and free iambic meters, as in the entrance song) alternate with three-line groups of iambic trimeters spoken by ETEOCLES. The excited CHORUS is again contrasted with the calm though not necessarily good-tempered ETEOCLES, as he tries to lessen their panic; the fact that the lyric stanzas decrease from five to three lines may indicate partial success in this, and in fact, a kind of compromise is reached in 233; until then there is clear disagreement between the CHORUS who rely on the gods and ETEOCLES who favors action. See Introduction, page 6 and footnote 13.

204 Once more the CHORUS is impressed by noises and reflects this in its language: *ton harmatoktupon otobon otobon/hote te sûringes eklangxan*—clattering changes to different sounds.

205–207 The text is unfortunately quite uncertain here, and in 212–13, 221–22; I have in general, but not quite exactly, followed Murray's OCT[2].

206–207 *guiding-gear . . . that steer them:* the Greek word *pêdalia* means "steering paddles."

208 *sailor:* i.e., especially the helmsman-captain, who must not desert his post at the stern and rush to the bow, even if statues of protective deities are there. On this persistent nautical metaphor, see Introduction, pages 18–19.

211 The CHORUS insists that it was not running away but rushing to seek divine protection; significantly it uses the word *prodromos* (rushing ahead), with which it described the Argive cavalry in 80; for a similar matching of dangers without and within, see 111 and 191.

212 *these old statues:* probably primitive wooden images.

hailstorm of stones came thundering down on the gates;
then it was that, roused by fear, I begged the gods
to keep watch over our town. 215

ETEOCLES Our walls—pray that these keep off enemy spears!
Thus the gods will save us. Yet, as for gods,
gods of a captured town leave it, they say.

STROPHE 2

CHORUS *Never, during my lifetime, may the deities*
assembled here desert us; may I never see 220
our city ravaged throughout by an army
that devours it with hostile fire.

ETEOCLES *Don't call on gods, I ask you, while your plans*

---

213 Slingers as well as chariots and horses—the same fears as in the entrance song, 150–59.

216 Gods are not enough; one needs something more substantial, like good walls (note that *stegein,* [*keep off*] possibly implies "be watertight"; see 234, 797, 1009, and *Suppl.* 135). Besides, the skeptic adds, when there is no more *quid pro quo,* gods are said to abandon a city. This idea of desertion was not rare; Rose gives several references (his commentary on 218); a good example is found in the prologue to Euripides' *The Trojan Women* 26–27: "For when desolation comes on a city with its evils, sickness comes on the divine; it would no longer be honored"; see also Aeneas' statement in *The Aeneid* 2. 351–53: "They are gone, all of them, abandoning their shrines and altars, those gods through whom this kingdom stood; it is a buried city that you are trying to help." Besides this, ETEOCLES seems to have doubts about the gods' ability to defend the city.

217 *Thus:* cf. 4, "the credit goes to god."

223–235 In this passage the opposition between ETEOCLES and the CHORUS is made obvious, especially since significant phrases begin the various responses: *Don't call on gods* (223); *there is still a divine power* (226); *This is men's job* (230); *It's the gods* (233). The last passage introduces a compromise, which ETEOCLES is probably glad to accept. But he is practical and honest enough to warn them that worse may come; and his reference to men dying will prove only too pertinent.

mean trouble; Obedience, you know, is Good Luck's
mother, wedded to Salvation, they say. 225

ANTISTROPHE 2

CHORUS *True, but there is still a divine power, looking down,*
and often when a man is distressed, helpless
and in deep misery, his view overcast
by lowering clouds, it rescues him.

ETEOCLES This is men's job, to offer sacrifice 230
and appeal to the gods when the foe strikes.
Yours is silence, to remain home, inside.

STROPHE 3

CHORUS *It's the gods that grant us life in a free city,*
though the enemy force is held off by our walls;
what resentment can be roused by that? 235

ETEOCLES I don't begrudge your honoring of gods.
But, to avoid making our townsfolk cowards,
make yourself calm; don't show excessive fear.

ANTISTROPHE 3

CHORUS *It was when I heard that strange clattering noise*
that I shuddered with fear, and up to the citadel, 240
this place of reverence, came in flight.

227–229 Probably a picture of a storm at sea—again the persistent nautical metaphor; for the powers of gods to help distressed mariners, see *Homeric Hymn to the Dioscuri* XXXIII, 6ff, and a later derivative, Theocritus 22. 8ff. For ETEOCLES there will be no such rescue.

230–232 See above, 200–201. Lines 230–31 are especially appropriate to ETEOCLES himself.

236 *gods:* ETEOCLES actually says *daimonôn genos* (the breed of deities), somewhat derogatory, as in 188 *gunaikeiôi genei* (womankind) and 256 *gunaikeion genos* (women! what a breed!).

239–241 The CHORUS repeats the reason for its rush to the citadel, only to be warned that they may have more to weep for.

ETEOCLES *Well then, don't if you hear of men dying or wounded, rush into wild lamenting!*
This is what war feeds on, the blood of men.

CHORUS *I tell you, I do hear horses snorting!* 245

ETEOCLES *Well, don't let your hearing prove too obvious!*

CHORUS *The town's very earth groans, under this siege.*

ETEOCLES *Doesn't it suffice that I take care of this?*

CHORUS *It scares me; the crash at the gates grows louder.*

ETEOCLES *Do keep quiet; say nothing like this in town.* 250

CHORUS *Gods assembled, do not abandon our walls!*

ETEOCLES *Confound you, keep quiet, restrain yourself!*

CHORUS *Gods of our town, keep me free from slavery!*

245–263 The CHORUS still has not learned; once more noises put it in a panic. A quick line-by-line interchange between the CHORUS LEADER and ETEOCLES makes him lose his temper again, so much as to provoke a brief spark of spirit in the CHORUS LEADER (257), immediately apologized for. A final harsh rebuke by ETEOCLES apparently subdues the CHORUS; and ETEOCLES, who knows the right thing to say (line 1), shows them the right kind of cry and prayer to utter, and then, practical as always, he tries to reassure them by naming himself as the seventh defender—salvation for them but, as it turns out, disaster for himself.

245 *I tell you, I do hear:* In Greek *kai mên akouô ge,* prosaically "furthermore I hear actually." This repeated emphasis serves to replace effects that in the modern theater could be produced offstage. (See my comments on the thunder and earthquake of *Prometheus Bound* in *Classical Philology* 46 [1951], 237–39.) ETEOCLES scornfully repeats the verb: "Well, although you hear, don't hear!" (see 202).

247 *earth groans:* see Introduction, pages 19–22.

248–257 Familiar attitudes—ETEOCLES' self-sufficiency, the CHORUS' fear of noises and dependency on gods—lead to a sharp interchange (256–57).

251 *Gods assembled:* the deities whose statues are in the orchestra; the Greek word used here, *sunteleia,* implies a group brought together for some specific purpose. It is noticeable that the CHORUS LEADER does refer to the city walls but puts the gods first.

ETEOCLES *It's you that enslave me and the whole town!*

CHORUS *Almighty Zeus, turn your weapons on the foe!* 255

ETEOCLES *Zeus—women! what a breed you created!*

CHORUS *Yes—wretched, like men of a captured city!*

ETEOCLES *More ill-omened words? While you grasp the statues?*

CHORUS *When courage goes, panic seizes one's tongue.*

ETEOCLES *Please, I ask you, grant me one slight favor.* 260

CHORUS *Please tell me quickly; perhaps I'll understand.*

ETEOCLES *Be quiet, you wretch! don't frighten your friends!*

CHORUS *I am quiet; I'll face what comes with the rest.*

ETEOCLES *This I prefer to your former outcries.*
Now, next, moving away from the statues, 265

---

257 The CHORUS LEADER reacts sharply: "We are no worse off than the *men* of a captured city!"

258–259 *ill-omened words:* since the point of touching a statue was to attract the deity's attention to an appeal, the CHORUS LEADER's words —more a statement than a prayer—might have disastrous effects. She realizes this and apologizes.

260–263 *Please:* almost with clenched teeth ETEOCLES, in mock politeness, asks "a favor"; the innocently polite answer of the CHORUS LEADER is met with an abrupt order, as abrupt as our "Shut up!" This quiets the CHORUS LEADER, but she ends with what is an ominous mutter: "Well, I won't be the only one to suffer!"

265 ETEOCLES wishes to get the CHORUS away from the various statues to prevent further "ill-omened words"; we recall the ritualistic use of *euphêmeite*, literally "speak favorably," implying "or else, keep quiet," and Horace's *favete linguis*; in solemn ceremonies silence is better than saying the wrong thing. So the CHORUS LEADER's words, "I am quiet" are preferable to inappropriate utterances. But the playwright-producer had another practical purpose; the CHORUS had to be brought together for the coming stasimon (287–368).

make a better prayer, that the gods join our fight,
and, when you have heard my prayers, you must shout
"Hallelujah!" the joyful, holy cry
people raise at sacrifice to give courage
to their friends; get rid of your fear of the foe! 270
Here and now, to our land's divine guardians,
lords of the fields, watchers of the market place,
to Dirce's springs, Ismene's stream, I swear,
should things go well and the city be saved,
we shall, reddening their hearths with sheep's blood, 275
[with slain oxen for the gods we address,]
set up trophies, spear-won spoils of the foe,
hung before the doors in their holy shrines.
Echo this prayer without excessive wails
to the gods, with no wild, futile gaspings! 280
These will not help you to escape your fate!

---

266 *join our fight:* in Greek "be our fighting-allies" (*xummachous*); ETEOCLES asks them not merely to pray against disaster, but to pray that the gods take an active hand in the struggle along with men; the word *xummachous* reflects his view that the Cadmeians must fight, not merely depend on gods (cf. note on 4). In a later play Agamemnon arrogantly commends the gods for being his allies (*Agamemnon* 811).

268 Consisting of four words this line throws into contrast the CHORUS' whole attitude: *ololugma* (a joyful cry), *hieron* (sacred), *eumenê* (beneficent), *paiônison* (sing in triumph). "Hallelujah" is not a Greek cry, but it surely gives the right effect. I have substituted "people" for "Greeks" in 269.

271–278 ETEOCLES offers a ritualistic prayer; it may be significant that here he addresses civic and local gods only. There is some textual difficulty in the passage, and line 276 is omitted by many editors; the text followed here is Murray's OCT[2].

273 Dirce was the most renowned of several springs whose waters fed the river Ismene, which flowed past Thebes; according to Euripides, *The Phoenician Women* 825–27, Dirce formed two contributory streams. Pindar's house was near the fountain of Dirce and he speaks of it as a source of poetic inspiration (*Isthm.* 6. 74).

281 Here, as often, by what is sometimes called "dramatic irony," a

I myself, as seventh, will lead a crew
of champions to face the foe heroically
at our seven gates; I'll go and place them,
before a flurry of foaming stories comes 285
with news to inflame us at this crisis.

ETEOCLES leaves.

STROPHE 1

CHORUS *I obey; but fear will not let my thoughts lie quiet;*

---

character's words recoil on himself. For demonstration we need only look at ETEOCLES' last words in the play (719); and it should be noted that the CHORUS LEADER ends in 263 with the same phrase as is used here at the end of ETEOCLES' sentence, *to morsimon* (that which is fated).

282–283 *a crew of champions:* an effort to reproduce the Greek *antêretâs* (counter-oarsmen); see also note on 593. ETEOCLES here leaves his position as steersman, a fatal step.

285 *foaming stories:* the Greek adjective *takhurrhothous* (swift foaming) recalls the nautical image; along with *phlegein* (inflame) it offers a kind of oxymoron, while also recalling the flaming courage of the attackers.

287–368 *First choral song.* After ETEOCLES leaves to resume his arrangements for defense, the CHORUS sings the first stasimon. In the first strophe and antistrophe it voices its fears roused by the Argive attack and begs Zeus and the city's gods for protection, dwelling on the richness of the land and the citizens' gratitude. Then the CHORUS depicts vividly the horrors of a captured city. In each of the four remaining stanzas the girls comment on what most affects them —the fate of captured women: a general picture (326–29), unmarried girls like themselves (333–37), mothers and babies (348–50), and after a brief glance at older slave-women (358–59), young women in slavery (363–68). General devastation and plundering fill the rest of the ode, with ominous comments on the conflict of man with man. Most striking is the third antistrophe (357–68), where destruction of the city is seen in terms of land's grown products (see especially 360–62) and where—the last picture in the ode— the CHORUS thinks of the dreadful future in captivity of girls like

close, pressing on my heart,
deep anxieties kindle a burning dread
of the force that surrounds our walls 290
like snakes that threaten young things;
this is the terrified fear for nestlings,
if they get such fearsome bedfellows,
that attacks an all-timorous dove.
Some foes are now near our battlements 295
in full force, fully assembled,
moving up—what will become of me?—
others, attacking on every side,
are pelting the men of my town
with rough, jagged slingshots. 300
Whatever the means, Zeus-born gods,
grant our city and our warriors,
sprung from Cadmus, salvation!

ANTISTROPHE 1

What land, what soil will you get to replace this, better
than ours, if you abandon 305
to our enemies this deep-rooted earth

---

themselves. They have hidden their fear only until Eteocles is out of earshot; yet although vivid in description, they are somewhat calmer; appropriately, the dochmiac meter is almost entirely absent.

289 The fire image may result from Eteocles' "inflame" in 286.

291–294 The surrounding army is like a snake coiled around a nest, resembling the bird-devouring snake whose actions Calchas interpreted as relevant to the siege of Troy (*The Iliad* 2. 308–16). The picture might also evoke thoughts of Eteocles' family in the words "fearsome bedfellows," quite apart from the obvious reminiscence of the Cadmeian serpent. In Greek the sentence is a masterpiece of word order: snakes, children, excessive fear, bad bedfellows, a trembling dove—a crescendo of excitement.

299 Reading *polîtais* (at our citizens) rather than Murray's *polîtai* (nominative).

304ff Another appeal to the self-interest of the gods.

306 The fertility of Boeotian soil was celebrated.

and Dirce's waters, by far
best of the streams we drink from,
best of all that come from Poseidon,
whose waters embrace the earth, 310
or come from the children of Tethys?
As you think of this, guardians of our town,
our own gods, cast on the foes around
our walls a destructive panic,
folly that makes men drop their shields; 315
hurl it on them, so that you win
glory among my townsfolk!
And thus, be my city's saviors,
with your firmly established power,
answering my shrill appeals! 320

STROPHE 2

How pitiful that a city so ancient as this
should be hurled down to Hades, a spoil of warfare,
enslaved, crumbled into ashes,
by Achaeans, at heaven's command,
brought to ruin unworthily! 325

309–311 Rivers are called the children of Oceanus and Tethys in Hesiod, *Theogony* 337; here Poseidon seems to be identified with Oceanus by the use of the attribute "earth-embracing."

314 *destructive:* actually "man-destroying," which may have overtones of the Laius-Oedipus-ETEOCLES-Polynices picture.

315 *drop their shields:* actually "drop their weapons"; but since the shield was one of the first things a runaway was likely to drop (see Archilochus, Alcaeus, Anacreon, and Horace) and since shields are so prominent in the play I have made the word specific.

321*ff* This strophe and its antistrophe set their tone by the initial words, "pitiful" and "tearful."

so ancient: literally *Ogygian*, a term of uncertain origin generally to mean primitive, primeval; Euripides calls the gate near Onca (486–87) Ogygian in *The Phoenician Women* 1113.

322 *hurled down to Hades:* an obvious quotation of *The Iliad* 1. 3: "Many were the valiant souls that [Achilles] hurled down to Hades."

Pitiful that captured women should be dragged away—
alas! young and old alike—
hauled, like horses by their forelocks,
clothes ripped from their bodies, while a cry
rises from the city laid empty 330
as its stocks are ravaged in a turmoil of shouts!
Yes, I foresee a dreadful fate, and shudder.

ANTISTROPHE 2

Tearful, too, that girls not ready to wed, though blooming,
should be taken without proper rites and have to leave
their homes for a hateful journey! 335
Why, one who is dead, I tell you,
fares better than such as these!
Many are the disasters one must face, alas!
when a city is laid low.
One man captures another, one man 340
murders; some start up fires, and smoke
pollutes the whole of the city.
With maddening inspiration, people-destroying,
defiler of Righteousness, comes the War God.

STROPHE 3

There is tumult throughout the town; in a closing ring 345
comes the hunting army.

326–329 A similar picture of women dragged off by their hair occurs in *The Suppliants* 430–32.

331 *its stocks are ravaged:* literally, "the booty perishing"; *lâis* or *lêis*, used here, generally refers to cattle or movable objects; the girls include themselves in such booty.

333–334 The text tradition here is chaotic, though the sense is clear; the picture of the dreaded future recurs at the end of the ode.

340f Hints of a duel may be seen in these lines.

345–346 *a closing ring:* literally "approaching (is) a towered fence"; Aeschylus probably uses a hunting metaphor from the practice of enclosing the prey in an area within a net and so making them more vulnerable; "towered" (i.e., military) clarifies the metaphor (see note on 64). Verrall's idea that there was an encircling rampart with towers is unthinkable.

By the sword of one man
another is slaughtered;
the screams of infants at their mothers' breasts
with their blood streaming down, babies
not yet weaned, fill the air. 350
There is plundering, bloodily akin to such rampage;
bargains are made—lucky sharing with lucky,
unlucky calling on unlucky
in a wish to have them as partners, all
wanting to get not less, not the same as the rest, but more. 355
When things are like this,
how can one see ahead, with reason?

ANTISTROPHE 3

Every kind of growing crop, cut down, falls to the ground
and brings bitter grief
when it falls; and sour is
the look in housekeepers' eyes,
when, profusely, in reckless confusion, 360
earth's products, utterly wasted,

---

348 *screams:* the word used here (*bremô*, verb, with *bromos*, noun) is used elsewhere for the sound of waves (85) or wind, the clash of objects or weapons (slingshots, 213), the snorting of horses (476; cf. 463); when applied to men it denotes angry noise (Tydeus in 378); the cries here are almost nonhuman. It should be noted that the *bromos* outside is now matched by *bromos* inside the city (see note on 110).

351 A tremendously concise line: "and plundering, blood-kin of rampages"; the two phenomena are personified and related, like smoke and fire in 494 or dust and mud in *Agamemnon* 494–95.

352–355 This picture suggests the rivalry of ETEOCLES and Polynices, especially after the use of *homaimones* (blood-kin) in 351.

355 This line ends with the word *lelimmenoi* (yearning for); the same word, in the singular, ends 380, effectively describing Tydeus.

356 The text is unclear; I translate Rose's suggestion *logôi*; the statement could have relevance to ETEOCLES' rational planning.

357*ff* On this picture and its relationship to the mother-earth image, see Introduction, page 22.

are swept away in torrents.
The slave-girls, still young, find new troubles facing them—
the misery of bedding as a captive
with a man who has the good fortune 365
of an enemy who has conquered—
this is all they can look for, meeting a duty at night-time
to complete their sorrows,
one wave of grief piled on another.

LEADER OF FIRST SEMICHORUS *Now here, I think, comes the scout from the front,*

---

362 *in torrents:* Greek *en rhothiois* (see note on 7); "spilled like water," Rose; Verrall thought of wine as well as grain.

363–368 The girls are ostensibly talking about other people, slave-girls, but they undoubtedly have their own future danger in mind. Textual difficulties, some doubt concerning syntax and the meaning of the last word in the ode, make interpretation uncertain. The translation is based on a possible, composite text with a different suggestion than the usual for the tantalizing last word.

367–368 If one realizes that the Greek word *elpis* does not necessarily mean "hope," but rather "expectation," one will avoid regarding the "night function" as "death." The last word, *epirrhothon,* has been interpreted as "helper" (against woes), "abetter" (of woes), "mocker" (of woes). But the root *rhoth-* has occurred several times in the play, always associated with noisy waves—in fact, as recently as 362. I find it difficult to avoid the implications of this usage; and I interpret *epirrhothon* as meaning "with an additional wave." (Cf. the triple-crested wave of 760.) In any case, this word, immediately preceded by "sorrows," creates a formidable phrase with which to end a choral song.

369–719 *Second episode.* No reason is given for the simultaneous appearance of the SCOUT and ETEOCLES, nor for their decision to meet on the acropolis. Such matters would be of little importance to a dramatist who could have a messenger and Agamemnon appear immediately after a last beacon is seen at Argos (admittedly after an intervening choral ode) or who could suddenly transform Delphi into Athens (*The Eumenides*).

The CHORUS, dividing into semichoruses for the occasion, bring us back to earth with the first words of their two utterances: *ho toi katoptos* (well, here you have the scout); and *kai mên anax hod' autos* (besides, here's the prince himself).

Two lines in this passage defy translation (371 and 374), although the poet seems to have given special attention to them: line 371 says, "with eagerness speeding the axle-boxes of his feet"; are we to say his legs moved like pistons, like clockwork? line 374 seems to mean, "the eagerness of this man too does not match his feet." A fascinating aspect of these lines is their similarity in verbal pattern and the possible implications. They begin alike: *spoudêi, spoudê;* and end alike: *podôn, poda;* reference to feet, especially with the rare reference to Oedipus in this part of the play (only in 203 hitherto) makes one wonder how far Aeschylean word-play could go. In any case the two characters are closely linked here; as before, the SCOUT is ETEOCLES' man; he came as quickly as he could, and ETEOCLES could hardly come fast enough.

It seems to me unlikely, as some editors have suggested (and as the manuscript reading occasionally seems to imply—cf. notes on 408 and 472), that ETEOCLES enters with six defenders whom he has already chosen; three had already been assigned to their posts (449, 473, 505; and perhaps 553); no sensible leader would withdraw them from their posts; and it is noticeable that no word is addressed to the defenders throughout the scene. It has been suggested to me by E. A. Havelock that the later production, which I assume introduced the two sisters, may have featured the champions on the stage with a few appropriate textual changes. Although this is possible, the specific statement of 447 remains a difficulty (see note on 447).

There must however be a small group of attendants, some to take word to the defenders chosen but not yet assigned, and at least two to help ETEOCLES into his armor (675ff).

We must remember that ETEOCLES does not know who the seven attackers are to be. There is no real stage action in the scene, merely the rhetoric of the SCOUT, ETEOCLES' answers, and the CHORUS' interjections. But there is increasing dramatic tension as ETEOCLES by his right decisions with appropriate comments gradually isolates himself as opponent to Polynices. The city is not entirely forgotten—at least by the CHORUS—since its fate is linked with that of Laius' family; but as the play develops the emphasis lies on that family and its survivors, especially ETEOCLES who must expiate the family's wrongdoings.

bringing us news, dear friends, some fresh report; 370
eagerness drives his feet at a rapid pace.

The SCOUT enters from one side, while ETEOCLES approaches from the other.

LEADER OF SECOND SEMICHORUS *Here too comes our ruler, Oedipus' son,*
in good time to hear the messenger's words—
eager, too, and nothing slows up his pace.

ETEOCLES enters.

SCOUT *With firsthand knowledge of the enemy's plans* 375
I shall tell what gate each was allotted.
Tydeus, already near the Proetid Gate,

375–376 The collocation of precise knowledge, stressed earlier by the SCOUT (40, 67), and decision by lot is significant in view of ETEOCLES' efforts to make the right choices.

377 Tydeus, son of Oeneus of Calydon, had sought refuge with Adrastus at Argos as a polluted murderer. Adrastus purified him and gave him his daughter in marriage. In the attack on Thebes, as described here by Aeschylus, he was killed by Melanippus. This is a simplification of a more elaborate version of Tydeus' death, according to which Melanippus wounded Tydeus but was himself killed either by Tydeus or Amphiaraus; the latter cut off Melanippus' head and handed it to Tydeus, bidding him gulp down the brains; Tydeus did so, thereby disgusting Athena who might otherwise have saved his life. Amphiaraus' suggestion was due to his hatred of Tydeus for encouraging Adrastus to attack Thebes. Though Aeschylus does not mention these details, the picture of Tydeus is consonant with it: an animal-like creature (381), madly ravenous for battle (380), violently at odds with Amphiaraus (382), who attacks him with reproaches that imply much of the more elaborate story (571–75). See note on 572.

Proetid Gate: the name seems to be connected with Proetus, a king of Tiryns, but the implications are not known. Perhaps Aeschylus' propensity for word-play induced him to set this Proetid Gate first (*prôtai*), especially since the last and most significant gate had a numerical name, the Seventh. (In Euripides, *The Phoenician Women* 1134, the last gate, where Adrastus the commander-in-chief

is growling; he must not cross Ismene's stream,
says the seer; the victims are against it.
So Tydeus, furiously craving battle, 380
with the vicious threat of a snake's noon-day hiss
strikes with fanged taunts at "wise seer, Oeclides,
who cringes before death and battle, the coward!"
With cries like this he shakes his triple crest,

---

took his stand, is called the Seventh.) The names of two other gates suggest their location: the Electran (eastern or southern: see note on 423) and the Borrhaean (northern: see note on 527). It is reasonable to suppose that the Scout listed the gates systematically, following the circuit of the walls. Certainly the sixth (Homolean), seventh, and first (Proetid) gates were in close proximity, since Amphiaraus at the Homolean Gate could address his remarks to both Tydeus and Polynices. See notes on 423, 460, 487, 527, and 570.

378 *growling:* see note on 348.

379 *the seer:* see note on 382.

380 *craving battle:* see note on 355; along with *lelimmenos* (craving) Aeschylus uses another participle, *margôn,* which also suggests ravenous hunger. Tydeus is, in fact, little more than an animal (381–82, 393–94).

381 *noon-day hiss:* the scholiast on this passage says, "You see, that is when he is maddest." Tydeus is one of the snakes that surround the city (290–91).

382 *Oeclides:* Amphiaraus, son of Oecles, a renowned prophet at Argos, who joined the expedition against his will (see note on 568).

383 *cringes:* the word used, *sainein,* is applied to a dog that wags its tail and fawns before its master, perhaps to avoid punishment; it seems to imply insincerity (see *Agamemnon* 798, 1665, *The Libation Bearers* 420); later, Eteocles uses the word when he refuses to cringe before approaching death (704).

the coward: for rebuttal of this charge, almost spat out by Tydeus at the end of the line, see below, 616–17.

384 The start of this line resembles that of 391 (*toiaut' aûtôn; toiaut' alûôn* (shouting thus; raving thus); we may assume that his shouts are madness.

his helmet's towering mane; beneath the rim 385
of his shield clanging bronze bells ring terror.
He has on his shield this haughty device—
a sky blazing with stars, carefully wrought,
and, brilliant in the center, the full moon,
our oldest star, the eye of night, shines forth. 390
Raving like this in his braggart array
he yells threats by the stream, wanting battle,
like a bridled horse, furiously chafing,
eagerly waiting for the trumpet's sound.
Who will you put there, at the Proetid Gate, 395
the way once opened, as a sure champion?

ETEOCLES *The array of a man—that I'll never fear;*

---

386 The line itself clangs: *khalkêlatoi klazousi kôdônes phobon.* The whole picture suggests the restlessness of Tydeus himself.

387 We pass from shouts, triple crest, and bells to the shield's symbol; it is described as arrogant, haughty—which sets the tone for most of the following descriptions.

388–390 The shield may be dark blue with a silver-colored boss and studded with stars. Lines 389–90 offer a good example of word-positioning: the sentence begins with *lamprâ* (brilliant), and ends with *prepei* (is conspicuous).

392 *wanting battle:* see 380.

393–394 *furiously chafing, eagerly waiting:* the manuscripts have here at the ends of 393 and 394 *katasthmainôn menei* (panting awaits) and *hormainei menôn* (is eager awaiting). Editors frequently offer a substitute for *menôn* (see OCT[2]), apparently disliking the repetition; but for Aeschylus, so fond of word-play, this interlocking cross-rhyme is thoroughly appropriate. The picture is that of a horse at a race, for which the signal was the sound of a trumpet (Sophocles, *Electra* 711). Some editors see the metaphor continued in 396 ("the gates once opened"), but this is dubious. Nevertheless, the picture recalls the beginning of the entrance song (79).

396 *sure champion:* the SCOUT's last word here is *pherenguos* (a surety, guarantee), significantly placed; it is used again by ETEOCLES in 449, by the SCOUT in 470, and is applied to the stout city gates by the MESSENGER in 797.

397 *array:* this, the first word in ETEOCLES' answer, shows his contempt.

and no wounds are dealt by shield-devices;
crest, bells!—these do not hurt without a spear.
And this night-sky you speak of on his shield 400
sparkling with heaven's stars—found on his shield,
well, some one may find his wild hope prophetic!
For if death's darkness does fall on his eyes,
the bearer of this arrogant device
will see the symbol fully justified: 405
it does foretell violence—to himself.
To face Tydeus I'll post Astacus' son,
a hero, to defend the gateway here;
of right good birth, he thoroughly respects
Decency and abhors arrogant words. 410
To shun base acts, never prove coward, this is
his wont. From the Sown Men whom Ares spared
rises his stock; true son of this land is
Melanippus. Ares' dice may set the outcome,

---

398 This idea is said to have been borrowed from Alcaeus, but it must have been commonplace, like our "Sticks and stones may break my bones," and so forth.

403 Possibly a Homeric reminiscence (cf., for instance, *The Iliad* 4. 461: "and [death's] darkness clouded his eyes").

405 *justified:* in Greek, *epônumon* (fitting its name).

407 *Astacus' son:* Melanippus (see note on 377), one of the true Cadmeian aristocrats, the *Sparti* or Sown Men (412; see Introduction, pages 19–20). Megareus, the third defender, is another of the Sown Men (474).

408 *gateway here:* reading *tônde*, which refers to the gates, not *tonde* (OCT[2]), which would imply that Melanippus was on stage.

411 *To shun . . . acts:* involves the word *argos* (not-doing), a pun on the enemy's name.

412–414 Here Ares has an equivocal position, ancestor and protector of the Cadmeians, but at the same time god of warfare, in which one must depend on luck (414); ETEOCLES, the soldier, understands the facts of war. On *true son of this land,* see Introduction, pages 19–20.

but true Duty to his kin calls the hero 415
to shield his motherland from enemy spears.

STROPHE 1

CHORUS *Well then, we pray that our champion may prove successful*
with heaven's favor, since duty to his city
sent him to help us; but I shudder at the blood
that is shed in the deaths of men who fight 420
for their friends! Oh, the sight of it!

SCOUT So be it! may this one win heaven's favor!
Next, Capaneus won the Electran Gate,
a giant this one, bigger than the man
described, and his boasts are more than human; 425
with wild threats at our walls—heaven grant they fail!—
he says he will sack our town, god willing
or god not willing; not even the crash
of Zeus' bolt on the earth will hold him back;
such lightning flashes with their thunderbolts 430
he likens to the sun's heat at midday.
His sign is an unarmed man bearing fire,

---

415 *Duty to his kin:* a duty defied by Polynices, who nevertheless claimed to have *Dikê* (Justice, Duty) on his side (644–48).

417–421 The CHORUS' interjections are mostly in dochmiacs (see above, pp. 38–39) offering a good lyric contrast to the iambic narrative. It seems to recall ETEOCLES' warning about possible bloodshed (242–44) and express their fears in ominous terms.

422*ff* After an "Amen" repeating some of the CHORUS' words, the SCOUT describes Capaneus, a gigantic blasphemer, not so animal-like as Tydeus, but certainly hardly human (425). He was the son-in-law of Iphis, Adrastus' fellow ruler in Argos.

423 *Electran Gate:* named after Electra, sister of Cadmus (Pausanias 9. 8. 3); perhaps it was an eastern gate facing the "beaming sun" (*êlektôr*), as Verrall suggested.

424*f* Tydeus is described in *The Iliad* 5. 801 as a short man but a warrior.

430–433 To meet the thunderbolt, a mere nuisance, Capaneus—or the man on the shield—needs no more than a flaming torch; *as weapon* represents the last word in the line and in the sentence.

a flaming torch in his hands as weapon,
and gold letters declare, "I'll burn the town!"
Against this man send—but who will face him, 435
withstanding such a braggart fearlessly?

ETEOCLES *Here one gain breeds another with interest;*
you know, when men have foolish ambitions
their own words often clearly betray them.
Now Capaneus makes threats, is ready to act 440
disdaining the gods; trying out his tongue
in foolish glee, mere mortal, up to heaven

433–436 The SCOUT stops short; he cannot think of a worthy opponent for this monster. But ETEOCLES has the answer—though actually legend has it that Zeus took the matter into his own hands, destroying Capaneus with a lightning bolt (see Euripides, *The Phoenician Women* 1180–86, and Sophocles, *Antigone* 127–33).

437 We do not need to replace the manuscript's *kerdei* (profit) by *kompôi* (boast) as in OCT[2]. ETEOCLES means: we profit from Tydeus' blasphemy, and here comes further profit as interest; as Verrall put it, "better and better!" The last word in the line is *tiktetai* (is produced, in a biological sense); while the regular word for "interest" is *tokos*, a related word, the choice of verb here is conditioned by the poet's general imagery (see Introduction, pp. 19–22).

438 The contrast between men (438) and gods (441) is emphasized by word juxtapositions: *mataiôn andrasin phronêmatôn* (for men involved in foolish ambitions, 438) and *kharâi mataiâi thnêtos ôn* (with a joy foolish for one who is mortal, 441). ETEOCLES actually introduces his statement with *toi* (you know, let me tell you), a particle that often introduces a piece of proverbial lore.

441 *trying out his tongue*: in Greek, *apogumnazôn*, almost "stripping for action." Since throughout this scene Aeschylus frequently has the two characters (and the CHORUS) link their speeches with what precedes—especially ETEOCLES, who wherever possible takes descriptions of the opponents and shrewdly turns them to Cadmeian advantage—*apogumnazôn* must play on the *gumnon andra purphoron* (an unarmed man bearing fire) of 432.

he launches at Zeus his loud-swelling boasts.
On him I know full well, with justice's aid
will come the true fire-bearer, Zeus's bolt, 445
no mere symbol like the sun's midday heat.
He faces a man—yes, one slow to talk,
but fiery of heart, brave Polyphontes
standing there, sure defender, by favor
of Artemis Protector and other gods. 450
Now, name another and the gate he got.

ANTISTROPHE 1

CHORUS *May he perish, this violent threatener of our town!*
may the thunderbolt's blast hold back his onrush
before he leaps into my home, and from my quiet

---

443 *loud-swelling (kumainonta)*: an almost inescapable metaphor for the sea-girt Greeks, but also natural in view of one of the dominant images in this play.

444 *I know full well:* on ETEOCLES' growing confidence see Introduction pages 8–9.

447– As usual the divine is coupled with human agency.
450 *slow to talk:* a translation different from the usual one; the word *stomargos* is generally translated "garrulous," "talkative," and applied to Capaneus; I doubt that the application is possible in view of the sentence structure, and I think that the word refers to Polyphontes, who is "fiery of heart," a match for Capaneus, the "fire-bearer." Then what quality does *stomargos* imply? There is word-play on Argos, as in 411, where Melanippus was described as "no doer of base acts"; here Polyphontes is "no user of words."

faces: the Greek has a perfect tense: "[Polyphontes] has been stationed," a statement impossible if Polyphontes came on stage with ETEOCLES.

449 *sure defender:* see note on 396.

449– One of the scholiasts asserts that Polyphontes was a priest of
450 Artemis.

451 The sound pattern of this line implies some kind of emphasis, probably confident sarcasm: *leg' allon allais en pulais eilêkhota.*

452– The CHORUS naturally picks up the thunderbolt motif, and now
456 to the thought of fearful bloodshed (419–21) they add their personal fears.

maiden abode with the arrogant might 455
of his spear takes and despoils me!

SCOUT *Very well: [the next one chosen at the gates*
follows;] the third man is Eteoclus;
from the upturned bronze helmet leaped his lot,
to hurl his men against the Neïstan Gate. 460
His horses fret in their headbands, as he wheels
back and forth; they want to rush on the gate;
from their nose-gear comes an outlandish whine
as the proud snorting of their nostrils fills it.
His shield's design is proud and grand in style: 465
an armed man on the rungs of a ladder
attacks an enemy fortress, bent on
destruction; he too shouts in lettered words
that not even Ares could dislodge him.

---

457 An unnecessary line, generally omitted because of grammatical and metrical weaknesses.

458 *Eteoclus:* this man seems to be a nobody, created to fill the place of Adrastus, who in this version of the legend does not attack any of the gates. Eteoclus himself has little personality, though he has a blasphemous shield and his horses recall Tydeus with their outlandish noises.

460 *Neïstan Gate:* the meaning of this name is not known, though the fifth-century lexicographer Hesychius states that the word *nêista* means "lowest" or "furthest." For its geographical position, see note on 377.

463–464 This must have been a splendid opportunity for an articulate actor, especially the second three-block line: *phîmoi de sûrizousi barbaron bromon/muktêrokompois pneumasin plêroumenoi*—hissing, booming, and sputtering! It should be noted that *bromon* (whine) at the end of 463 is an emendation of the manuscript's *tropon* (manner or style), almost certainly justified because of the scribe's catching sight of *tropon* at the end of 465 and to the influence of the cliché *barbaron tropon* (in barbaric fashion).

469 It was particularly foolhardy to blaspheme Ares while attacking Ares' own city (104–5), and a natural choice to meet the challenge would be one of the Sown Men.

So, send against this man one you can trust 470
to ward off from our town slavery's yoke.

ETEOCLES [*I shall send this man at once; god go with him!*]
One has been sent, in fact, whose boast is "Action!"
Megareus, Creon's son, from the Sown Men's breed;
never will frantic horses' whinnying 475
and snorts scare him; he will not quit the gate.
No, by death he'll repay his land for nurture,
or take two men and the town on the shield,
come home, and deck his father's house with spoils.
Now, some other man's boast! don't spare your words! 480

---

472 Many editors feel that this line is inconsistent with the next one. If both lines are kept one must assume that ETEOCLES started to say, "I shall send this man . . ." and then remembered that he had already done so. I find it difficult in that case to account for the demonstrative *tonde* (this man). The word is used as evidence by those who believe that the champions came on stage with ETEOCLES; this is hardly possible if we keep 473. Murray brackets 473; I prefer to cut out 472, as suggested by Murray in his first edition.

473 *boast is "Action"*: literally, "has his boast in his hands."

474 Megareus, according to Euripides, *The Phoenician Women* 942–44, is as true-blooded a noble as any of the Sown Men could be. Tiresias tells Megareus' father Creon: "You are what we have left of the Sown Men's lineage that have pure blood on the mother's and the father's side, you and your sons" (Megareus, called Menoecus in Euripides' play, and Haemon). Like Melanippus (415–16), he will repay his land for nurture (477); ETEOCLES notes the possibility of death in both cases, but here stresses the probability of victory (478–79). In Sophocles, *Antigone* 1303, Megareus is mentioned as dead by Eurydice as she laments the death of Haemon.

475–476 *frantic, snorts:* these words represent Greek words related to the Greek of "furiously" and "growling," which are applied to Tydeus in 380 and 378. See note on 463.

478 *two men:* Eteoclus himself and the man on his shield.

480 A troublesome line whose meaning and syntax have disturbed editors. An attractive suggestion was made by Rose (*Commentary,*

STROPHE 2

CHORUS *Again I pray: may the defenders of my home*
win success while our foes meet with misfortune!
As they howl their braggart threats against the city
in madness of mind, so may Zeus
the Requiter look down on them in anger. 485

SCOUT Next, the fourth: assigned the gate that is near
Onca Athena, he stands there shouting,
Hippomedon, a mighty bulk and form.
A huge threshing-floor—his round shield, I mean—
scared me as he whirled it—I can't deny it! 490
The designer must have been no cheap one,
whoever put on the shield its emblem—
Typhon shooting out from his fiery mouth
a murky flame-flecked smoke akin to fire;
serpents' coils at the surrounding border 495
base the sign firm on the shield's hollow belly.

---

p. 201), who regards the line as a scornful statement that Megareus might make when he brought his dead enemy's spoils to his father's home: "Now brag over others; don't begrudge my boasting!" But the line must be attributed to ETEOCLES, serving as a transitional statement like 451.

485 *Requiter:* Greek *nemetôr* (apportioner, divider), which anticipates later emphasis on the division of property between ETEOCLES and Polynices.

486–496 Like Capaneus Hippomedon is gigantic and impious, and like him he positively invites Zeus's retaliation. Typhon (Typhaon, Typhoeus), son of Tartarus and Gaia, a fire-breathing monster, tried to depose Zeus; he was blasted by Zeus's thunderbolt and buried beneath Etna. He had a hundred snakes growing from his shoulders; his head must, then, have formed the emblem in the center, with snakes in relief serving as clamps to fasten it to the body of the shield.

487 For Onca Athena, see note on 164; cf. 501.

489 Another Aeschylean explanation of a metaphor; see note on 64.

494 See note on 351.

He himself, with a war cry, war-possessed,
holds fierce Bacchic revel, glaring terror.
Such a man's attack demands good defense;
for here at our gates Terror stands bragging. 500

ETEOCLES *Well, first, Onca Pallas, our town's neighbor*
near this gate, hating human arrogance,
will shield her nestlings from this chilling snake,
while Hyperbius, Oenops' valiant son,
already picked, meets him man against man, 505
ready to learn his share in destiny
at a crisis—in form, spirit, and war's skills
beyond reproach; Hermes made a shrewd match.

497–498 *He himself:* a frightening figure, embodied Terror (500), as irrational in his frenzy as a Bacchant. Euripides developed this picture in *The Phoenician* W*omen* 784–97, where the Chorus describes Ares as revelling in blood, *paramousos,* out of harmony with Bacchic rites, in a dance *anaulotaton,* without music. In *The Aeneid* 7. 385–405, 580–84, Vergil shows the Latin women excited by Amata in a Bacchic revel that leads to a demand for war.

497 Noise is characteristic of these attackers, even if colorless Eteoclus has to depend on his horses' equipment and the figure on his shield (463–64, 468); see 378, 381, 426, and contrast 410 and 447.

501–514 Again divine help is available—Onca Pallas (see 164 and note) and Zeus, and skeptic or not, ETEOCLES does not reject such aid. Nonetheless he stresses human action: man will face man (505), and the Cadmeian is a good match for his opponent (507–8). The fact that this man is already chosen and has on his shield Zeus, unconquered conqueror of Typhon, is a godsend, gift of Hermes, the god of luck. Not only ETEOCLES, but even the CHORUS, becomes confident (521).

503 For this picture, suggested perhaps by Typhon's serpents but also related to the Sown Men, see 290–94 and note.

504 The scholiast felt it necessary to note that *huperbios,* an adjective implying "exceptional strength," was used here as a proper name.

505 Here and in 509 we have an anticipation of the duel between ETEOCLES and Polynices; see 674–75.

508 *Hermes,* god of a lucky find (*hermaion*), cooperates here with good reasoning (*eulogôs*).

For as man meets man here as enemy,
both will besides present as foes on their shields 510
deities: one has fire-breathing Typhon,
Hyperbius has Father Zeus on his shield
in firm stance, a blazing bolt in his hand;
and who has ever seen Zeus defeated?
[So this is the way the gods' favor lies: 515
we are with the victors, our foes the vanquished,
if Zeus really is mightier than Typhon—
and the men confronted may well fare thus— 519
so Hyperbius, to match his emblem, 518
may find a savior, Zeus, here on his shield.] 520

ANTISTROPHE 2

CHORUS *I firmly believe that one who has on his shield*
Zeus's foe, the unlovely form of a power
earth-born, whose likeness is hated by mortals—yes,
and also by the long-lived gods—
will fall and smash his head before our gates. 525

SCOUT *So be it! Now I speak of the fifth man*

---

511 *deities:* the Greek word *theous* occupies just this position: end of the sentence, start of a line with enjambement, and therefore likely to be emphatic.

514 A strong ending, which encourages the CHORUS to cry *pepoitha*, "I firmly believe." The standing Zeus with arms spread, ready to hurl a thunderbolt, is a familiar archaeological pose.

515–520 This passage, frequently regarded as an interpolation (as in OCT[2]), adds little to, and in fact weakens, ETEOCLES' confident statement in 514. The firm assertion of the CHORUS in 521 demands an ending like 514, not the hesitation of 520.

518 Lines 518 and 519 are usually transposed as here.

521–522 The Greek here has *antitupon*, which, while it can mean "adversary," recalls the *tupos* (form) of 488; it is literally a countermold or countertype and thus recalls Aeschylus' use of *antêretâs* (counter-oarsmen) in 282–83.

526–562 The fifth attacker is young and handsome, but his looks are deceptive; they cover an impious and savage nature. He defies Zeus and, in insulting bravado, has chosen the Sphinx as his shield-device, apparently in the hope that he will become a lively center of attack

stationed at the fifth, the Borrhaean Gate,
right by the tomb of Zeus-born Amphion.
He swears by the spear in his hand, firmly
revering it more than a god, more than life, 530
that he will raze Cadmus' town, in spite of Zeus.
So shouts the mountain-ranging mother's son,
fair of face, part man, part boy, but warlike;
over his cheeks is spreading fresh soft down,

(543–44); and in gratitude to his adoptive motherland he plans to fight as vigorously as any of the Sown Men of Cadmeia. To face him ETEOCLES would welcome divine assistance (550), but as usual, he has a man whose skill needs no boasting to help it. God willing (562), the Sphinx will be defeated. If the prince seems less confident than in his previous speech, the CHORUS is terrified and prays for divine protection.

527–528 The Borrhaean Gate is presumably the northern gate (cf. Boreas, the North Wind, and see note on 377). The casual reference to Amphion indicates how carefully Aeschylus has eliminated material that has no place in the Cadmeian story; a familiar legend made Amphion and his brother Zethus builders of the walls of Thebes. In Euripides, *The Phoenician Women,* Parthenopaeus is stationed near Zethus' tomb.

530 *more than life:* literally, "more than his eyes."

531 Parthenopaeus repeats almost exactly the positive part of the oath sworn by the Seven, but he shows his impiety by adding defiance of Zeus in a clever piece of syntactical legerdemain: a clause ending *astu Kadmeiôn biâi* (the city of the Cadmeians in violation of the Cadmeians) is extended by the addition of *Dios* (and in violation of Zeus).

532 *mountain-ranging mother's son:* Parthenopaeus, son of Atalanta. She had been exposed by her father Iasus, was nursed by a she-bear, and led the life of a huntress until she was acknowledged by her father. Parthenopaeus' father was Melanion, who defeated Atalanta in a footrace by throwing down golden apples and thus delaying her.

533 *fair of face:* in Greek, *blastêma kalliprôiron* (a scion with fair prow), obviously untranslatable and a tantalizing recall of the two major images in the play. Iphigeneia is described as being *kalliprôirou stomatos* (of a fair-prowed mouth) in *Agamemnon* 235, where

as youth develops the thick growing hair; 535
yet, harsh in mood, with no youthful softness,
glaring fiercely he takes his stand nearby.
With a bold emblem, too, he faces our gate;
our city's shame is on his bronze-wrought shield,
the rounded protector of his body— 540
a raw-devouring Sphinx, neatly riveted there;
he wields this shield with the bright embossed shape
that holds beneath her a Cadmeian, one man
to take the shower of missiles hurled at him.
Now that he's here, he surely will not deal 545
in petty fights, wasting the long trip he made,
Arcadian Parthenopaeus; this man,
an alien repaying Argos for nurture,
hurls threats at our fortress. Heaven grant they fail!

---

there is also a nautical context. To sea-going Greeks the adjective may have become colorless, but the poet gives it a new life.

part man, part boy: the Greek *andropais* (man-boy) refers to one no longer a boy but fully grown.

536 *harsh:* in Greek *ômon* (crude, raw); the word links Parthenopaeus with the Sphinx *ômositon* (raw-devouring), 541.

with no youthful softness: literally, "by no means suiting the name of maiden" (the *parthenos* in his name means "maiden"); this description, along with the evidence of 532, is enough to indicate who the attacker is.

537 *glaring fiercely:* literally, "with a Gorgon-look," which is an appropriate reference to Medusa, whose face was beautiful but had a petrifying effect.

545–546 This is not a man who deals only in local products; he travels in pursuit of his business, and he feels under an obligation to his adopted country. He will therefore be a formidable opponent.

547–549 These lines have been regarded as totally spurious, partially spurious (549), or as misplaced. Murray, in OCT[2], set them between 537 and 538, probably feeling that the attacker's name should come early as in the other cases. But the descriptive hints given in 532ff make his name obvious; and the reference to Arcadia in 547 explains the phrase "long trip" in 546. Murray also bracketed 549 as a repetition of 426; but repetition is no sign of weakness; the "naturalized" Argive can threaten Cadmeia as well as any other attacker.

ETEOCLES *I wish—heaven help us!—they'd suffer their own threats;* 550
then they'd perish, utterly, miserably, 552
they themselves and their unholy bragging. 551
There is one to meet this Arcadian you name,
no braggart—his hand sees what must be done—
Actor, brother of the man I just named. 555
He will allow no tongue's flow without deeds,
unchecked, to enter our gates and breed mischief
nor allow that abhorred ravenous beast
[carried in effigy on a foe's shield,]
to come inside. The beast will blame her carrier 560
for her heavy hammering at the city's walls.
With heaven's help, perhaps my view will prove right!

STROPHE 3

CHORUS *The messenger's words pierce me to the heart;*
the hair of my head is standing on end.
As they hear the bragging of these braggarts, 565
these infidels, may the gods, if they be gods,

550–552 ETEOCLES picks up the SCOUT's wish and amplifies it, hoping that the enemies' threats may recoil on themselves, literally, "would that they might get what they are purposing, at the hands of the gods." In the translation I have adopted a suggestion that 551 and 552 be interchanged; they offer good Greek and better sense.

554 This man has skilled hands that will do what is needed instinctively.

556–557 *without deeds, unchecked:* an effort to reproduce the effect of the Greek word *ergmatôn*, which may mean either "deeds" or "dikes." Obviously, talk is not enough to get Parthenopaeus into the city if his talk faces action; and the "flow" demands barriers. There is a hint of the growth metaphor in "breed" (*aldainein;* see 12).

559 There are good grammatical reasons for bracketing this line.

561 The hammering the Sphinx will take from spears, matches the hammering she suffered when the shield was made; twice is too much.

562 As at the start of the speech, ETEOCLES considers divine help.

563–567 ETEOCLES is less confident, and the CHORUS is terrified in contrast to their attitude in 521–25.

destroy them here in my land.

SCOUT *Sixth I'll name a virtuous, valiant man,*
a prophet, mighty Amphiaraus.
At the Homoloean Gate, his station, 570

---

567 *here in my land:* an excellent introduction to Amphiaraus, who was blasted into the ground by Zeus outside the city. See following note and note on 587.

568 So far we have had a sequence of attackers who are marked by a brutality and impiousness that lead them to confidence that they can conquer, god willing or not. Even if they are powerful—and in spite of ETEOCLES' skeptical attitude about the gods—the odds (the will of the gods) are against the attackers. Or at least it appears so until Amphiaraus is mentioned; this man is far from blasphemous and, though reluctant, will try to prove himself a warrior. If impious men are dangerous, this man is more so (595–96). Amphiaraus is a man who needs no bragging or shield-device to inspirit him; consciousness of his own worth is enough (590–94), and this gives ETEOCLES pause for thought (597–619).

Amphiaraus, a human being prepared for by Parthenopaeus, who has at least the semblance of a human being, also serves to focus attention on the family of Laius and Oedipus by his comments on Polynices (580–86).

Eriphyle, daughter of Adrastus and wife of Amphiaraus, had been bribed by Polynices to persuade her husband to join the expedition. He was a reluctant member and felt particular hostility toward Tydeus, whom he regarded as instigator of the war. In the final battle, to save him from death at the hands of an enemy, Zeus opened up the earth in front of him and he sank from sight (cf. note on 587).

569 This line ends with a familiar Homeric idiom: *Amphiareô biân* (the might of Amphiaraus, i.e., *the mighty Amphiaraus*); 571 and 577 end *Tudeôs biân* and *Poluneikous biân.* This repetition is called by Rose "careless even for Aeschylus." But actually Aeschylus is deliberately setting one kind of hero against another; he enlivens a poetic cliché.

570 *Homoloean Gate:* the variety of explanations offered by ancient commentators for this name suggests that they knew no more than we do. Most explanations refer to some place called Homole that was associated with the family of Niobe or Amphion.

he loudly reviles the mighty Tydeus:
"You murderer, you city-confounder,
Argos' foremost instructor in trouble,
the Fury's awakener, Bloodshed's henchman,
Adrastus' counsel and guide to trouble!" 575
Then turning to mighty Polynices,
your own blood brother, inverting his name,
splitting it in two, stressing the last part,
he addressed him, and let fly with these words:
"Do acts like this really win divine favor? 580
noble to tell and hear of in later times?
that your father's town and its native gods
be sacked by your foreign invading force?
The mother-source—who can block that justly?
And your father's land—if your ambition 585

---

571 The hostility between Tydeus and Amphiaraus was indicated earlier in 382–83.

572–573 At Argos, Tydeus (see note on 377) aroused not only the Fury of his own murderous behavior but the Fury of the house of Laius; along with Polynices, he stirred up Argos to war and bloodshed. I find it difficult not to associate much of this picture with Oedipus, whose arrival at the Cadmeian city was so calamitous.

576–579 This passage is full of problems, both of text and interpretation, discussion of which has no place here. Line 578, for which different interpretations are given, is sometimes cut out as mere repetition—needlessly, I think, since Aeschylus often tries to explain himself; some editors would also cut out 579. Clearly Amphiaraus broke Polynices' name in two, inverted the order of the component parts, and attacked him as *neikos, neikos polu* (strife, strife aplenty). Cf. 658 and 830; and for similar serious play on names, cf. *Agamemnon* 687–90; Sophocles, *Ajax* 430–31; Euripides, *The Phoenician Women* 636–37.

582–587 The implications of the father-mother passage are discussed in the Introduction, pages 20–22.

583 *foreign:* this factor made Polynices' attack even worse.

584 *mother-source:* see Introduction, page 21.

and spear take it, can it be your ally?
I myself, I know, will enrich this land,
a prophet buried in enemy soil.
So, to battle! I expect an honored death."
Thus spoke the prophet. His shield is quiet— 590
for all its bronze—with no surface device;
not mere show, but true courage is his aim,

---

586 For a verbal reminiscence of this line, see Euripides, *The Suppliants* 246 (quoted in note on 602); cf. also *The Persians* 792: "the land itself is their ally."

587–588 Amphiaraus makes no threats and, in contrast to Parthenopaeus (531), refers only to the second part of the Seven's oath; but here the sense is different, since he will enrich the land as a benefactor buried there.

Amphiaraus was deified and worshiped as a divine oracular hero with a shrine at the spot where he was said to have vanished, on the road to Potniae near Thebes. According to one story Amphiaraus gave the Thebans a choice: they could either accept him as a prophet or as an ally in war; they chose the latter. (In *Ol.* 6. 17 Pindar speaks of Amphiaraus as eminent both as a prophet and as a warrior.) Similarly, in *Oedipus at Colonus* Oedipus frequently states that his presence after death will be a blessing to the city that welcomes him. Cf. lines 1524–25: "Thus shall [my burial spot] provide you with defense better than many [native] shields and the spears of neighboring allies."

589 Amphiaraus uses a characteristic Greek method of emphasis, the combination of two negatives—"a not dishonorable death"; the implication is that others will meet a dishonorable death.

591 *for all its bronze:* the shield is as serviceable as that of any of the others, but without bells or extravagant devices. The quiet nature of Amphiaraus' shield is also noted by Euripides, *The Phoenician Women* 1111–12.

592 This line has an epigrammatic quality in Greek: *ou gar dokein aristos, all' einai thelei* (for not to seem, but to be the noblest is his wish). Plutarch, *Aristides,* Chapter 3, says that when it was uttered at the production of the play in 467 B.C., the whole audience fixed its gaze on the famous "Aristides the Just." Aeschylus may well be indulging in another word-play (one of noblest ap-

as he digs deep in a rich, fertile mind
and develops the fruits of good counsel.
Here a wise, brave opponent should be placed, 595
to my mind; devout men are dangerous.

ETEOCLES *How wretched is the luck of men that links*

---

pearance, *aristos eidos*, being suggested by *Arist-ides*). For the popularity of the line, see Rose, *Commentary, ad loc.*

593–596 The influence of the growth metaphor makes itself felt in 593–94, and in 595 "opponent" represents *antêretâs* (counter-oarsmen), ETEOCLES' word in 283.

596 If a man is likely to have the help of the gods, the Cadmeians certainly need good defenders.

597–619 The situation of Amphiaraus makes ETEOCLES realize that chance may involve even the innocent in the destruction that falls on the evil, simply through association. But as he concentrates on the problem of defense, his own words do not make him think of his own position—even Amphiaraus' reference to Polynices seems to have passed over his head—or the relationships of his own family in general. After mentioning what must have been two commonplace examples, he refers specifically to Amphiaraus, implying, however, that the prophet's fate is something that the gods will attend to. All the same, human precautions must be taken, and Lasthenes is posted at the gate. But ETEOCLES is even less confident here than in 562 and less skeptical than in 4; it is not merely a matter of who gets credit for success but where the success comes from; the negative stage is reached in 719.

It is interesting here to recall an account of the expedition of the Seven given in connection with Amphiaraus in Pindar, *Nemean* 9, 16–27. Zeus and his thunderbolt are frequently referred to in Aeschylus' play, but they are far more significant in the Pindaric narrative: Zeus tried to dissuade the Seven from their venture by a thunderbolt, but they disregarded the omen; their expedition was thus even more impious; Amphiaraus, however, was spared from the general disgrace, since although he had to perish, his end came when Zeus's thunderbolt split the earth so that Amphiaraus was swallowed up.

597–598 In the context of this play these lines invite consideration of ETEOCLES' relationship with Polynices, especially since ETEOCLES denies that Polynices has any justice on his side (662–72).

the fate of the just with the impious!
In all man does, evil relationships
are the worst evil, with crops not to be reaped. 600
[Sinful folly has for its harvest—death.]
A devout man, who has boarded a ship

599–600 Evil communications not only corrupt good manners (Euripides, frag. 1024 Nauck[2]) but may bring disaster. So it was with the relationship of Oedipus' mother with Laius and with Oedipus (750–57).

601 A good line, but to be deleted as an illustrative parallel which slipped into the text.

602–608 The general sentiment recurs in Euripides, *The Suppliants* 223–24 and 226–28, when Thesus tells Adrastus that a wise man would not associate just people with the unjust, because god regards their fates as linked and destroys even the innocent associates of the sinners along with them. The speech of Thesus has several reminiscences of Aeschylus' play, of which one deserves note: *kâpeit' egô soi summakhos genêsomai* (and so shall I become your ally?) in 246 must surely be based on Aeschylus' line 586: *halousa pôs soi summakhos genêsetai* (having been captured, how shall it be your ally?). The question, "Why do the innocent suffer?" is an old and continuing one: it figures prominently in Solon, frag. 1 Diehl, 29–32, where the vengeance of Zeus is likened to a violent windstorm, which is totally devastating and quite indiscriminate (19–21), and there is a lively protest at such unfairness in Theognis 373ff ("Why, Zeus, I am surprised at you!").

The vignettes in 602–8 suggest the characteristic examples, the *topoi*, that must have been familiar to writers generally—poets, rhetoricians, philosophers, satirists. Euripides, frag. 852 Nauck[2], notes the danger of sacrificing with the wicked and of going to sea with them; in Euripides, *Electra* 1355, Castor warns against sailing with perjurers; Horace, *Odes* 3. 2. 26–30, speaks of the danger of sharing a house or of setting sail with the impious; Hesiod, *Works and Days* 238–47, asserts that a whole city or a whole fleet may suffer for one villain; Xenophon, *Cyropaedia* 8. 1. 25, says that it is preferable to go to sea with men of acknowledged piety, but Antiphon, *On the Murder of Herodes*, 82–83, points out, in view of the acknowledged fact that the presence of the impure would cause disaster, that his own presence on a ship or at a sacrifice never caused anyone trouble.

with seamen hotly bent on some mischief,
may well drown with the god-detested crew;
or a just man, with fellow citizens 605
who reject strangers and forget the gods,
may be trapped along with them, unjustly,
and fall, struck by god's all-inclusive scourge.
Just so, this seer, the son of Oecles,
a man both wise and just, devout and brave, 610
a mighty prophet, linked with impious men
who with brash utterances defy good sense
in their fine parade too long for return,
by Zeus's will must be dragged down with them.
Now, I think he will not even hit the gate— 615
not that he's a coward or faint of heart;
no, he knows that he must die in battle,
if fruit is to come from Loxias' words,
a god who keeps quiet or speaks to the point.
Still, to face him, our mighty Lasthenes, 620
a watchman harsh to strangers, will be sent;
mature of mind, he shows youthful vigor

---

604 *god-detested crew:* the word *genei* (group) is used in a derogatory sense here as in 188 (*womankind*), 236, and 256 (*breed*).

608 *all-inclusive:* pictorially shown by Solon's windstorm that destroyed even the "fair handiwork of men" (see note on 602).

611–612 This picks up 597–98, but it also recalls the behavior of Laius and Oedipus who, as we shall see, acted in defiance of good sense.

613 Probably a suggestion of the road to death.

614 This three-word line begins with the will of Zeus (*Dios thelontos*) and ends with an impressive seven-syllable dragging verb: *sunkathelkusthêsetai* (will be dragged down along with them).

617–619 ETEOCLES apparently knows the prophecy relating to Amphiaraus' presence in the expedition, and in another growth metaphor he implies a belief in the words of Loxias-Apollo, while at the same time he characterizes the god as one who conforms to his own ideas: appropriate utterance is certainly what ETEOCLES approves (619 ends *legein ta kairia* [to say the appropriate things], as does 1). It is a fine irony that makes ETEOCLES comment thus on the merit of Apollo's words when the outcome of his utterance to Laius is still awaited (see 745–49).

and quickness of eye; his hand does not wait,
when a shield bares flesh to spear it at once.
But only god can grant success to mortals. 625

ANTISTROPHE 3

CHORUS *May the gods hear the prayers we justly raise*
and fulfill them, for our city's success,
making war's horrors recoil on our land's
invaders! May they be outside our walls when Zeus
blasts them with his thunderbolt! 630

SCOUT Next the seventh man, here at the seventh gate,
your own brother. I shall tell the curses
and prayers for ruin he hurls at the city:
"May I mount the walls, be proclaimed abroad,
shout a glad, triumphant song of capture, 635
meet and kill you, dying, if I must, with you;
if you live, may banisher be banished,
dishonored like me, requited by me."

---

623 An exasperating line beginning *podôkes omma, kheiri,* an extraordinary anatomical juxtaposition: "a foot-swift eye, and hand."

624 I read *dorei* (with the spear), a correction of OCT²'s *doru;* see Rose, *Commentary, ad loc.*

625 A rueful acknowledgment that man's wisdom cannot control everything; cf. the *dice* of Ares in 414.

629f This wish and 567 neatly bracket the picture of Amphiaraus.

631 We have had five impious monsters, against whom the Cadmeians must surely be successful if there is any right and reason in the world. But then comes a change: Amphiaraus, thought-provoking not only because of his virtues but by his references to the family of Laius and Oedipus. And yet mention of Polynices by Amphiaraus does not excite ETEOCLES; nor does the SCOUT seem conscious of the approaching crisis.

636 *kill you, dying:* cf. 697: both princes are conscious of Oedipus' curse, which is explained later.

637–638 This shows that Polynices has been banished, but we have no account of the reasons in this play; everything is presented from ETEOCLES' side. There is a preponderance of *t*-sounds in this passage that could represent angry "sputtering"; this continues in *toiaut' aûtei* (cf. 384), which begins 639.

Shouting thus he calls on his race's gods
and fatherland's gods to observe the prayers 640
of a true man of war, Polynices.
He has a newly wrought, well-rounded shield
with a twofold device fashioned on it—
worked in gold, a man pictured in armor,
escorted quietly by a woman 645
who, as the letters read, says, "I am Justice"
and "I shall restore this man; he shall have
his father's city and home to move in."
Such, then, are the devices of the foe.
Now, you yourself must pick the man to send; 650
my part—the reports—you will find well done—
yes, you yourself must choose the city's course."

The SCOUT leaves.

ETEOCLES *Alas, maddened by god and god-abhorred,*

---

641 *true man of war: pankhu Poluneikous biâ* (truly the might of a "much-fighter"); the phrase ends the line in the same way as in 569, 571, and 577 (see note on 569); there is a similar play on the name in 658.

642 The Boeotian shield was perhaps oblong, in contrast to the new, round type of shield.

647–648 Oedipus, too, had been an exile and returned to possess his father's home.

650 The similarity of 650 and 652 has caused some editors to delete 650. Rose would retain 650 but change the repetition in 652—quite wrongly, I think. The SCOUT notes that his "captain"—and possibly the CHORUS—is distressed; for some reason his carefully given news is disturbing, and he stammers and stumbles (contrast 67–68).

653–655 The city's captain cries out in realization of what he has hidden from himself so long; the gods, whom he has regarded so lightly, now show their power, as does his father's curse.

653 ETEOCLES acknowledges the power of something called gods; both adjectives apply to his family—offensive to Apollo since the time of Laius and maddened to irrational anger, except, he had felt, in his own case.

all-wretched is mine and Oedipus' race!
Ah me, now my father's curse is fulfilled! 655
But weeping and wailing have no place here;
we must not breed more unbearable griefs!
For him so well named—Polynices, I mean—
perhaps we shall see what his sign will fulfill,
whether gold-worked letters will restore him, 660
set on a shield with wandering of wit.
Now if Zeus's maiden child, Justice, stood
by his acts or thoughts, his boast might prove true;
but, neither when he fled the dark of the womb,
nor in his nursing, nor adolescence, 665
nor when the hair was gathering on his chin
did Justice look on him or acknowledge him.

---

655 The Greek has *patros dê nûn* (of my father, in fact, now); it amounts to something like, "This is it!"
curse: actually plural in Greek, and fragments 2 and 3 of the *Thebais* (see Evelyn-White) indicate that Oedipus cursed his sons more than once.

656 As usual Eteocles immediately gets down to business.

657 *breed . . . unbearable:* the language recalls the growth-family metaphors. What Eteocles probably means—as his character would suggest—is that he does not want to add the city's destruction to his own. By his own confrontation of Polynices he may avert this.

658 See 641.

659 "I have found answers to the other shield-emblems. What about this one?"

661 A line of assonances and the like (cf. 637–38); *ep' aspidos phluonta sun phoitôi phrenôn,* continued in 662: *ei d' hê Dios pais parthenos Dikê parên.* Eteocles is being emphatic here. In 662 there is another play on words, as if *Dikê* (Justice) were connected with *Dios* (of Zeus); in *The Libation Bearers* 949, *Dikê* is called *Dios korê* (Zeus's daughter), a flagrant pun, as use of the adjective *etêtumos* (cf. etymology) indicates. The line is reminiscent of Hesiod, *Works and Days* 256: *hê de te parthenos esti Dikê, Dios ekgegauia* (there is also maiden Justice, child of Zeus), where *Dikê* and *Dios* are juxtaposed.

Nor when he ravishes his father's land,
as now, do I think she will stand by him.
Why, then, in all justice would Justice be 670
falsely named, aiding an utter villain!
Convinced of this I shall go and meet him
myself; who else could have a better right?
Prince against prince, brother against brother,
as personal foes we'll meet! 675
Bring at once
my greaves, to shield me against spears and slingshots!

---

668 See 582–86 and the general implications of the Laius-Oedipus-wife-mother story.

670–671 *in all justice . . . Justice: pandikôs pseudônumos/Dikê,* three powerfully juxtaposed words, helped by the line break "all-justly falsely named/Justice." In view of 662 and the Hesiodic parallel cited there we see that the poet is saying, "then Dike has nothing to do with Zeus." For a similar comment on the failure of a name to be suitable, see *Prometheus Bound* 85–86: "with a false name [*pseudônumôs*] do the gods call you Prometheus [Forethinker]; for you yourself need forethought [*promêtheôs*]."

672 *convinced of this:* in Greek, *pepoithôs;* forms of this word were used by the CHORUS in its one moment of confidence (521) and in the description of arrogant Parthenopaeus (530), but the most significant use is that of ETEOCLES himself in 37, when he says, "these [scouts], *I know,* will not waste time; with their news no trickery will trip me." Now with the news clearly given, he firmly takes the matter into his own hands (note the strongly placed *autos* [myself], at the start of 673). Polynices has no *dikê* of any sort, but ETEOCLES has a special, complicated *dikê homaimôn* (cf. 415 and 477), a duty to his motherland, which involves family relationships.

673 *better right:* we must not forget that the situation is presented from ETEOCLES' point of view; but whatever the rights of the case, the general question of the city's danger is reduced to a personal feud (674–75), related to divine displeasure with ETEOCLES' family. The CHORUS' interest shifts—though not completely—from fear for the city to comment on and concern for the family of Laius. (On the change from generic to concentrated specific vocabulary in this connection, see Introduction, pages 25–26 and footnote 51.)

During the next verses attendants bring in ETEOCLES' armor.

CHORUS *Do not, dearest child of Oedipus, prove*
in mood like him who cursed so violently.
Cadmeians encountering Argives—that
is enough; such blood can be atoned for. 680
But if two blood brothers kill each other
like this, when can such pollution grow old?

ETEOCLES *If ill luck must come, it must come without*

677–719 In this scene we have an interchange of brief choral lyrics with short iambic passages as in 203–44; but here, in contrast to the earlier situation, the CHORUS tries to advise ETEOCLES. It urges him not to pollute himself by killing his brother; he must not be carried away by murderous passion; by caution, by avoiding personal pollution, he may, with god's favor, escape the Furies; the winds of Fortune may change. ETEOCLES, however, feels that his luck has run out; Apollo is continuing the anger aroused by Laius and by Oedipus' curse, which is now being fulfilled; the gods have abandoned him like a defeated city; his suppressed fears are now realized. He sees what lies before him, and he will meet it heroically.

ETEOCLES' resolution is given visible evidence if we accept the suggestion of Rose (*Commentary*, pp. 217–18)—later echoed by W. Schadewaldt, with minor variations—that we have here a dramatization of a heroic arming scene (e.g., Paris in *The Iliad* 3. 330ff; Agamemnon in *The Iliad* 11. 17ff; Achilles in *The Iliad* 19. 369ff). See the directions in the translation.

677 The CHORUS addresses ETEOCLES with affection, as in 203, as "child of Oedipus"; there is a certain ominous quality in the phrase, now that the crisis is approaching. The only other use of the phrase so far (372) may have involved minor connotations.

678 Probably refers immediately to Polynices, but can clearly involve Oedipus. (Some would translate: "him who was so bitterly denounced by you.")

681 *kill each other:* the Greek says "self-killing death"; the killing of one as close as a brother is regarded almost as suicide. See also 734–35, 805, 850.

683–685 ETEOCLES' only hope is to leave a good name; the importance of *kleos* (renown) is found throughout Greek literature, especially in sepulchral epigrams.

disgrace; such fame alone profits the dead;
but ill luck plus disgrace—that brings no renown. 685

ETEOCLES puts on the greaves.

STROPHE 1

CHORUS *Why so eager, my son? let no heart-consuming,*
war-craving folly carry you away! Cast out
evil passion at its start!

ETEOCLES *Since the affair clearly is sped by god,*
on, wind-borne, to Cocytus' waves, the goal 690
set for Phoebus-hated Laius' whole race!

ETEOCLES puts on the corselet.

ANTISTROPHE 1

CHORUS *Too ravenous is the yearning that urges you on*
to accomplish a man-killing of bitter fruit,
shedding blood not to be shed.

---

687 *war-craving: dorimargos* in Greek; it refers to the same kind of craving that characterized Tydeus in 380 and 393. The CHORUS here and in 692 compares ETEOCLES' spirit to a passionate love or desire (688, 692) which recalls the passion of Laius (750).

carry you away: things move quickly now; see 689 (is sped), 692 (urges you on), 698 (be urged ahead). The word used here suggests a wind or tide, and the nautical image is continued in ETEOCLES' answer. The CHORUS and ETEOCLES differ on what is responsible for this speed: it says he himself is responsible; he talks of Apollo and the curse. Surely the combination is what is disastrous.

689 *god:* ETEOCLES has come up against a situation that he cannot control, and he traces it back to its source.

690 *Cocytus* (River of Wailing): one of the five rivers that surrounded Hades, the Underworld, home of the spirits of the dead. The other four rivers were Acheron (River of Woe), Styx (Hateful River), Pyriphlegethon (Fiery River), and Lethe (River of Forgetfulness).

691 We go back to the start of the whole disastrous story. Note that ETEOCLES says, *Laius*' whole *race.*

692 *ravenous: ômodakês*, a word recalling Parthenopaeus (*ômon*, 536) and the Sphinx (*ômositon*, 541).

693f This could apply to Oedipus as well as to ETEOCLES.

ETEOCLES *My own cause this hatred; a father's black curse* 695
on my dry, undimmed eyes settles itself,
saying, "First comes profit, then later death."

ETEOCLES puts on the sword.

STROPHE 2

CHORUS *No, do not be urged ahead! You will not be called*
coward for faring well in life. Out of your home
the black-robed Fury will vanish, when from your hands 700
the gods receive sacrifice.

ETEOCLES *Gods? by now, it seems, they've abandoned me;*
the gift of my death is what they'd admire.
So why cringe any more before death's blow?

ETEOCLES picks up the shield.

ANTISTROPHE 2

CHORUS *Cringe now, when death stands before you. For*
destiny's 705

---

695 The line begins *philou (gar) ekhthrâ*, juxtaposing words denoting "loving," "beloved," or "one's own kin" and "hating," "hated"—a succinct commentary on the intrafamily hostilities.

696 Perhaps the curse has been with him so long that he has no tears left.

697 I take this disputed line to mean: "first you will kill Polynices, then die." Cf. 636.

698–699 Wise withdrawal from conflict will not be called cowardice (see 716).

699–701 I interpret this passage (which has a slight textual difficulty) to mean that by avoidance of wrongdoing and by propitiation of the gods ETEOCLES may personally escape the Fury. (There is almost a hint of the theme of *The Eumenides* here.) The final words, however, are unfortunately too applicable to ETEOCLES himself; cf. 230–31.

702–704 ETEOCLES seems utterly disillusioned; he feels like the captured city that he spoke of previously (217–18). The gods have withdrawn; what remains with him is the curse. But he will not cringe any more than Amphiaraus, who was falsely accused of cowardice by Tydeus (383).

mood may veer and just at the last moment alter,
and perhaps come upon you with a kindlier
breath; but as of now, it seethes.

ETEOCLES *Seethes? it has seethed over—Oedipus' curse!*
Only too true were the nighttime visions 710
I had, when my father's goods were divided!

ETEOCLES puts on the helmet.

CHORUS *Give heed to women, for all your dislike.*

ETEOCLES *Then say something practical; but be brief.*

CHORUS *Don't make this journey to the seventh gate!*

ETEOCLES *My purpose is keen; words will not blunt it.* 715

CHORUS *Yet god respects success, even a coward's.*

705*ff* The nautical metaphor again; for another use of the change of wind metaphor, see *Agamemnon* 219, where Agamemnon's mind veered. Reference to a possible change in destiny (*daimôn*) anticipates the last two words of what I regard as the essential ending of the "story"—*elêxe daimôn* (the Fury found its end), where the verb used can apply to the dropping of a wind (see note on 956).

709–711 ETEOCLES' consciousness of the curse has been quietly simmering (witness his nightmares); now it has come to a boil.

711 *goods were divided:* first hint in this play of the content of the curse; see 727ff, 788ff, 816ff, 903ff.

712 See 182ff. The last word in this line is *homôs* (nevertheless), very strongly placed.

713 *be brief:* ETEOCLES has no time, as usual, for useless words.

715 *keen, blunt:* another hint of the curse (succinctly given in Euripides, *The Phoenician Women* 68: *thêktôi sidêrôi dôma dialakhein* (with sharpened steel to divide the household). To the CHORUS' final pleas ETEOCLES gives three short answers: "my mind is now made up" (perhaps he picks up his spears here); "I must meet my fate in the heroic tradition; god's will is inescapable." The mortal has come to acknowledge the divine power on which the CHORUS has relied all the time.

716 The CHORUS seems to accept the *quid pro quo* skepticism of ETEOCLES' earlier comments. But he has a heroic concept of his duty.

ETEOCLES *No warrior will brook such an utterance.*

CHORUS *But, shed your own brother's blood—do you mean that?*

ETEOCLES *When god gives evil, man cannot escape.*

ETEOCLES leaves.

STROPHE 1

CHORUS *I shiver at the house-destroying* 720

---

718 *shed:* literally, "pluck"; perhaps a hint of the plant-growth metaphor.

719 Not a rare concept; see, for instance, Solon, frag. 1 Diehl. 64 (Edmonds, *Elegy and Iambus*, Solon, frag. 13): "the gifts of the immortal gods cannot be refused"; Theognis 1033–34: "the gods' destined gifts no mortal man will easily escape"; Theognis 1189–90: "and anxieties, when it is god who sends such pains, no mortal man will escape by propitiatory gifts." A lighthearted version of this old proverbial saying is found in *The Iliad* 3. 64ff, where Paris says that Hector should not criticize him for his good looks, "for, you know, the gifts of the gods are not to be thrown away."

ETEOCLES leaves with words considerably different from those of his first skeptical comment (4). In 281 he told the CHORUS that wailing would not help it to avert its fate; and he follows his own advice (656–67); in 625 he acknowledged that success was the "gift of god." He realizes that clearly now: the prince who decreed a public execution which a mortal would not escape (199), now finds himself facing a divinely ordered destiny that he cannot escape.

720–791 *Second choral song.* The center of this ode (third strophe and antistrophe) is occupied by a brief account of the sins of Laius and Oedipus and the CHORUS' fears of the results to ETEOCLES, Polynices, and the city. This section is framed by 742–49 (the utterance of Apollo and the source of vengeance) and 766–71 (comment on the disaster and curse that seem to attend eminent families). The CHORUS begins its song (720–41) in shuddering fear of the power of Oedipus' curse, gives the first (somewhat elaborated) account in this play of the curse, and laments the unabated activity of the curse and Fury. At the end of the ode (772–91) it notes the eminence and fall of Oedipus, his curse on his sons (explained more simply and specifically this time), and its fear about swift fulfill-

god who is like no other god,
full of truth in ill-foreboding,
a father's curse-invoked Fury;
I shiver at fulfillment of the wild
curses of Oedipus' demented mind; 725
for child-destructive strife here presses on.

ANTISTROPHE 1

A stranger gives out the allotments,
a Chalyb come here from the Scyths,
to arbitrate the family's goods,
a harsh, keen-tempered blade of steel; 730
it has granted land to dwell in,
as much as the dead can occupy,

---

ment. In this carefully framed ode immediate effects enclose the original causes.

721 *like no other god:* something more than human, but as the scholiast implies, not the usual gods, the givers of good. In the *Oresteia* this is remedied when the Furies become *The Eumenides,* the "Kindly Ones."

724–725 *wild . . . demented mind:* this suggests an element in the family of Laius that contributed to its destruction.

726 *child-destructive:* this has specific reference to ETEOCLES and Polynices, but like many phrases in the play it has wider application.
presses on: see note on 687.

727ff Now we learn what ETEOCLES' nightmares must have been.
stranger: this suggests that the family no longer has personal control of its fortunes.

728 The Chalybes, generally placed south of the Black Sea, were reputed to have discovered how to work iron; they are not actually Scythians (cf. 816), who lived north of the Black Sea; but even later, in *Prometheus Bound,* Aeschylus' Black Sea geography is hardly reliable.

730 The blade is called *ômophrôn* (savage-tempered), an adjective that recalls *ômodakês* of 692 and other words noted there.

731–732 A similar grim phrase is used of the Greeks who died at Troy and "occupied" the land there in *Agamemnon* 454.

but the rich, wide flatlands are denied them.

STROPHE 2

When brother murders brother
and they die, slain each by each, 735
and the dry dust of the earth
drinks up the blackened clot of murderous blood,
who will then provide cleansing?
who give ablution? Alas,
burdens of the household, new ones 740
mingled with the old evils!

ANTISTROPHE 2

Now a sin of long ago
comes, I say, with vengeance swift,
to the third generation;

---

granted: along with 727 this phrase implies a similar procedure to that which was followed when the Seven cast lots (55). ETEOCLES has to face a more serious casting of lots.

734–735 The Greek has *autokotonôs autodaïktoi* (in self-killing self-smitten); cf. 681.

736–739 For the irrevocable nature of blood spilled on the ground, see, for instance, *Agamemnon* 1017–21: "but when once there has fallen on the ground in death a man's dark blood, who will call it back by incantations?" *The Libation Bearers* 48: "what redemption is there when blood has fallen on the ground?" and *The Libation Bearers* 67: "the vengeful clotted blood will not flow away." This bloodshed started with the killing of Laius.

740–741 The chainlike succession of wrongdoing and punishment is, of course, basic to the *Oresteia*. Here there is an added touch in *new . . . mingled with the old,* with Oedipus' marriage as context.

743 *vengeance swift:* see the last words of this ode: "Fury swift of foot" (791).

744 *third generation:* Apollo gave three warnings (746), and the CHORUS speaks of a "triple-crested wave" of disaster (760). This suggests that the present third generation will see the end of the

it has waited ever since Laius defied 745
Apollo, who bade him thrice
at Pytho's earth-centered shrine,
from which come oracles, to die
childless to save his city.

STROPHE 3

But, yielding to his own foolish counsel, 750
he begot disaster for himself,
Oedipus who killed his father
and seeded his mother's
sacred soil, where he himself was reared,
accepting the bloody stock 755
that grew. He came from parents mated
by distracted frenzy.

Curse-Fury's activity; it will end with the deaths of ETEOCLES and Polynices. One is reminded of the importance of *Zeus tritos Sôtêr* (Zeus, third and Savior), in the *Oresteia,* where Aeschylus developed fully the concept of a third generation that meant salvation. He ends *The Libation Bearers* with reference to a triple wave of disaster. The derangement of Orestes, who had come to settle the problems in the house of Agamemnon, leads the Chorus to say: "Here, as you see, in the royal house a third successive storm, a family-bred blast, reached its sad end . . . now in turn there came as third from somewhere a Savior—or shall I say, Destruction?" Is Orestes a savior? Will he solve the family's problems or must the chain of disasters be continued? The reference is to the third of three libations poured, to Zeus the Savior, at the end of a banquet.

748–749 The ambiguity of this oracle has been suggested in the Introduction, page 2. In effect, the deaths of ETEOCLES and Polynices, sole surviving descendants of Laius and his wife in my view, ended the family curse. This particular warning of Apollo is not found in our extant Sophoclean works; its source is not known.

750 *foolish counsel:* a primary example of the impetuousness of the family of Laius.

753–756 For the metaphor in this passage, see Introduction, pages 19–22.

756–757 These lines must refer to Laius and his wife, since Oedipus was not the victim of *paranoia* when he married.

ANTISTROPHE 3

That sin, like a sea, brings waves of evil,
one sinking, another rising high,
triple-crested, surging around 760
the ship of state's timbers,
while between stretches a thin defense,
the mere thickness of a wall.
And I fear along with our princes
our city may perish. 765

STROPHE 4

For the fulfillment of curses uttered
long ago brings heavy requital:
but disaster passes by the poor,

758–763 A good example of the ship-of-state image, linking the family of Laius with the city; although the CHORUS is especially concerned with that family, the fate of the city—linked with the family in Apollo's warning—does not escape them.

waves: cf. the waves of the enemy in 114–15.

760 *triple-crested:* suggests the belief that the third wave was bigger than the two before it; cf. 985, and *Prometheus Bound* 1015: *kakôn trikûmia* (a third wave of evils). One is reminded of Tydeus' triple-crested helmet (384–85).

762–763 Cf. 216 and 234. What has happened to the CHORUS' reliance on defense by the gods?

767 *requital:* in Greek *katallagai*, whose precise meaning is disputed; but the word does suggest "exchange" or a "business payment"; it may conceivably also suggest "reconciliation," which would indeed be heavy—the princes' deaths.

768–777 The CHORUS implies that wealthy, eminent families are so susceptible to disaster that some kind of retrenchment is advisable. Similar ideas are found in the *Oresteia*, with the qualification that wealth alone is not the cause of disaster, but wrongdoing; cf. *Agamemnon* 750–60: "There is an old saying among mortals uttered long ago, that the great growth of a man's prosperity develops further growth and is not without result when it dies, and that a man's good for-

while over the stern must be cast
by men of substance 770
the excess of fattened wealth.

ANTISTROPHE 4

Consider: what man was ever so much admired
by the gods who share our city's homes
and the thronging crowds of his fellows
as famed Oedipus, who thwarted 775
the man-devourer,
the Sphinx, and rescued our land.

STROPHE 5

But when Oedipus
sensed the misery of his marriage,
wretched and overborne by grief, 780
his distracted heart led him

---

tune produces for his family unquenchable misery. Quite different from that of others is my own view: it is an impious act that later produces more impious acts that resemble their origin"; and *Agamemnon* 1008–13: "If in time part of the acquired wealth be heaved overboard in cautious fear with a well-calculated throw, the whole household will not sink under the excessive weight of its sufferings; the vessel is not submerged."

the poor: translation of Bücheler's excellent textual emendation. For the thought, cf. *Agamemnon* 773–78: "But Justice gleams in smoke-begrimed [i.e., small] houses and she honors the just man, while gold-bedecked mansions where the hands are polluted she leaves with eyes averted." Horace neatly sums up the philosophical cliché in *Odes* 2. 10. 5–8: "He who chooses the golden mean lives safely free from the squalor of a shabby home and in his prudence free from the envy aroused by a palace."

772–782 The theme, "How are the mighty fallen!" is fully treated in Sophocles' *Oedipus the King*.

774 *thronging crowds:* reading *polubatos agôn* (much-trod assemblage) for OCT²'s difficult *polubotos aiôn* (age rich in flocks?).

to commit a twofold evil:
with the hand that slew his sire
he banished the light of his precious eyes.

ANTISTROPHE 5

Then, against his sons, 785
in anger at their shoddy tending,
he launched bitter curses, and said
that with arbiter of steel
in hand they would someday divide
their goods. Now I fear it may 790
be fulfilled by a Fury swift of foot.

---

782 *twofold:* specifically refers to his self-blinding and the cursing of his sons; but the word is undoubtedly related to his two eyes and his two sons.

783 *slew his sire:* by implication this involves the "suicidal" intrafamily references already made; the hand that slew his sire has harmed himself—another link in the chain!

784–786 Textual difficulties cause problems of detailed interpretation; I offer the general sense.

786 *shoddy:* frankly, an evasion; in Greek the word is lost, but the sense is generally understood.

791 *swift of foot:* here, as elsewhere (371, 374), there is interest in words that refer to feet; the lame-footed Oedipus must have settled firmly in the thinking of Aeschylus and also of Sophocles (see Bernard M. W. Knox, *Oedipus at Thebes*, New Haven, Conn.: Yale University Press, 1957, pp. 182–83). I have some doubts, personally, about the translation of *kampsipous* (791) as "swift of foot"; I suspect that the often despised scholiast may have had a point when he translated *kampsipous* as referring to "that which contorts the feet of people being punished, for instance, that which binds the feet together to prevent running away." Reference is sometimes made to archaic pictures of running figures like Gorgons, strangely knee-bent creatures—fair enough! But the scholiast may have realized that Aeschylus could use and revivify a familiar term with pungent reference to context—the *kampsipous* Oedipus. Such connotations would enrich 371 and 374. Nevertheless, speed seems to be envisaged since we immediately learn of the curse's effect (792–802).

MESSENGER enters.

MESSENGER *Be of good cheer, beloved mothers' daughters!*
Our city has escaped slavery's yoke;

792ff *Third episode.* From here to the end of the play we are faced not only by many textual difficulties but also by the possibility that much of the text may be spurious, derived from later interpolations and additions. The interchange in lines 803–11, the CHORUS' anapestic introduction of ANTIGONE and ISMENE (861–74), and 1005–78 are especially suspect. Much of the suspicion is based on reluctance to admit that the sisters and the problems raised by ANTIGONE could be introduced at the end of the trilogy. I have discussed the matter above (Introduction, pages 22–25), but I should state my views briefly here: (1) I think that the sisters are alien to Aeschylus' version of the story; with ETEOCLES and Polynices the whole family of Laius was wiped out; references to sisters and their presence are impossible; (2) I cannot accept the idea that Aeschylus ended a trilogy with a question mark, posing another problem yet to be solved, though the solution arrived at—utter destruction of Laius' family—is like cutting the Gordian knot; a more satisfactory solution to a similar problem was arrived at later in the *Oresteia*; yet (3) I cannot completely condemn all the "spurious" passages as non-Aeschylean; except for 861–74, the lines seem to me to have been written by someone who knew his Aeschylus, and especially this play, well.

If ANTIGONE and ISMENE are to be discarded—quite possible, I think, until we reach 1005—we must consider who spoke 875–1004 (as well as 1054–78). Here I am indebted to the honest appraisal of Lloyd-Jones—especially honest since his article does not favor those who would curtail the ending of the play (see Bibliography, page 126). Except for 1026–53 I have eliminated ascription of speeches to ANTIGONE and ISMENE. I have assumed that the CHORUS divided and that much of the end of the original play was sung by semichoruses or semichorus leaders.

792 The MESSENGER may feel a kindly superiority to these scared creatures, but at least, unlike Oedipus, they were brought up by their mothers.

793 This might recall the recent Persian invasion.

fallen, brought low are those warriors' proud boasts;
the state now has fair weather, and for all 795
the waves' buffetings it has shipped no sea;
the walls hold tight, the gates had as bulwarks
champions whom we could trust in single fight.
Things go well for the most part—at six gates;
but the seventh awesome Apollo took, 800
Captain of Sevens; on Oedipus' house
he fulfilled Laius' ancient act of folly.

CHORUS *What further news do you have for our town?* 803

---

794 A fit end for the braggarts previously described; the line begins with *peptôken*, a fine emphatic word: "they are down, down and out!"

795–798 The MESSENGER employs the familiar nautical image, along with appropriate words like *stegei* (hold tight), 797; cf. 216, 234 and *pherenguiois* (trusty), 797; cf. 396, 449, 470.

796 The nautical image is assisted by the splashing noises with which this line begins: *pollaisi plêgais antlon* (under many blows sea-water).

799 The MESSENGER has tried to quiet the CHORUS' fears about the city —not quite successfully; see 843–44.

801 *Captain of Sevens: hebdomâgetâs* (leader of sevens; seven-leader), whatever it means, is another example of what Verrall called Aeschylus' "curious verbal ingenuity"; it refers here to the seventh gate but reflects Apollo's epithet *hebdomâgenês* (born on the seventh day).

802 *act of folly*: see 750.

803–811 It is generally acknowledged that this passage is a conflation of two different stage versions; concerning the original text, opinions differ. The OCT[2] gives a four-line version and a seven-line version; Verrall offers a two-line version. Here I attempt to make some sense out of the preserved text. The MESSENGER is interrupted three times by the excited CHORUS, but finally in 805 (transposed to follow 810 in the translation) he is able to state the matter bluntly, and the CHORUS' following question is picked up by the first word of his answer in 812–19. See note on 812.

MESSENGER *The town is safe; but the royal brothers—* 804

CHORUS *Who? what's that? I'm beside myself with fear!* 806

MESSENGER *Just be calm and listen! Oedipus' sons—*

CHORUS *What misery! I knew trouble would come!*

MESSENGER *I tell you plainly: laid low in the dust—*

CHORUS *They went so far? I dread it, yet tell me.* 810

MESSENGER *The men are dead, slain by each other's hand.* 805

CHORUS *So much akin that they slew each other?* 811

MESSENGER *Yes, too much akin in their destiny,* 812
that power which now consumes this hapless house.
Such are the joys and laments left with us—

---

804 *The town:* the MESSENGER, replying to "our town" in 803, tries to answer the question raised in the preceding ode; he, too, knows that Apollo's warning linked the city and Laius' family together. So he mentions "princes" (804); the CHORUS, perhaps wishing to hide the truth from itself, interrupts with "Who?" Its distraction (*paraphronô*, 806) is answered by his "be calm" (*phronousa*, 807); he is again interrupted, but at last he manages to state the case flatly.

807 *be calm:* the MESSENGER has the same trouble with the CHORUS as ETEOCLES had; perhaps 809 reflects his impatience.

809 Like the SCOUT earlier he tries to offer clear information.

811 *so much akin:* literally, "with hands so brotherly were they struck at the same time."

812 The CHORUS began 811 with *houtôs* (thus, so); the MESSENGER begins his answer with the same word. Lines 811 and 812 actually show considerable parallelism:

houtôs adelphais khersin ênaironth' hama?
houtôs ho daimôn koinos ên amphoin agân.

I do not see how these lines can be separated, no matter who their author may be.

destiny: daimôn, as in 705 and 960.

a city faring well, while the leaders, 815
the two princes, with forged Scythian steel
divided the sum of their possessions;
they shall have land—as much as burial needs—
by a father's curse haplessly swept away.
[The town is safe; but the royal brothers— 820
the earth drank their blood; they slew each other.]

The MESSENGER leaves.

CHORUS *O mighty Zeus, guardians of our city,*
you gods who firmly protect from harm
these Cadmeian walls:
shall I shout in joy my hallelujahs 825
since Salvation has left our city unscathed?
or weep for the wretched ill-starred brothers,
leaders in war, now dead and childless?

---

815 *faring well:* as in 4 and 77.

816–819 The MESSENGER knew the curse, too. For Scythian steel, see note on 728.

819 *swept away:* see note on 687.

820–821 Bracketed dubiously; they are kept by Verrall as the original answer of the MESSENGER; kept in the text, they form a clinching summary; and yet, *phoroumenoi* (swept away), the last word of 819, would be an excellent word to end with.

822 *Third choral song,* to 1004. The CHORUS begins with anapests, announcing their formal reentry into the action; the strophe, antistrophe, and possible epode that follow are written basically in lyric iambic rhythms. Lines 822–31 are deleted by Verrall.

823 *firmly:* represents the emphatic particle *dê* in *hoi dê* (who in fact).

825–829 The indecision of the CHORUS here reflects the twofold nature of the MESSENGER's news (815); it also, perhaps, anticipates a subsequent division of the CHORUS for different reasons.

hallelujahs: on this word, see note on 268.

828 *childless:* I see no other way of interpreting *ateknous.* See Introduction, page 24 and footnote 48.

who rightly fulfilled the sense of their names,
for truly renowned *and* source of much strife 830
they perished for their impious thoughts.

STROPHE 1

O black and consummating curse,
cast on the house by Oedipus,
anguish settles around my heart with chilling fear!
I raise a funeral dirge 835
in frenzy, as I hear of
blood-dripping corpses, ill-fated
victims. Truly ill-omened was
that duet of mated spears.

829–830 The manuscripts contain reference only to Polynices (source of much strife), a play on the etymology of his name, but the sentence demands that ETEOCLES also be mentioned; the supplement in OCT², *kleinoi t' eteon* (renowned truly), fits the need in both sense and sound-play (*eteo-klês*).

832–860 After its first indecision the CHORUS begins a lament for the sons of Oedipus; it still has some doubts about the city's future (843–44), but this disappears in the formal lament. And, in fact, in the present text the issue seems settled by 953–60.

832 The sinister power of the curse is now constantly emphasized; it seems significant that such references should pile up now in the later part of the play (655, 695, 700, 720–26, 766–67, 787, and *passim* subsequently) after a single mention near the beginning (70).

836 *in frenzy:* in Greek, *thuias* (a Bacchant). The same picture for irrational excitement is found in 498, describing Hippomedon. ETEOCLES had warned the CHORUS about the possibility of such bloodshed in 242–44.

838 *ill-omened:* in Greek, *dusornis* (with a bad bird, i.e., "bad omen"); this statement implements 597–99, where a bad omen (bird) produces evil relationships.

839 *duet of mated spears: xunauliâ doros;* the Greek word *xunauliâ* is usually interpreted to mean a "musical duet," derived from the word *aulos* (wind instrument); but the word can also mean "a dwelling together." We again sense the implications of 597–600.

ANTISTROPHE 1

It did its work and did not fail, 840
the father's invoked, uttered curse;
Laius' unbelieving counsels found fulfillment;
but still we fear for the town,
for god's warnings keep their edge.
O grief-laden house, your deeds are 845
beyond belief! Disaster has come
in fact, not mere prophecy.

The bodies of the princes are carried in.

Here we see self-evident proofs of the message,
a double cause for grief, double acts of valor,
evils of self-slaughter, a double doom, here 850
fulfilled in grief.

840–844 Oedipus' curse has been fulfilled; the exact fulfillment of Apollo's warning is still a matter of doubt. But factual evidence—the deaths of Eteocles and Polynices and the bringing of their bodies on the stage—seems to cause the Chorus to forget the city's possible danger. I do not see that Aeschylus had in mind any subsequent attack on the city; the worry is characteristic of the young Chorus.

844 A reflection of the "sharpened steel" of the curse.

847 *not mere prophecy: ou logôi* (not mere word). We have here a reflection of the developing Greek interest in the contrast between *ergon* (fact, deed) and *logos* (word, statement). The phrase here is justified by the *actual* introduction of the bodies of Eteocles and Polynices. There is a theatrical quality about the phrase: "I don't have to tell you! look for yourself!" Aeschylus exploited this trick in his *Prometheus Bound,* where after several preliminary indications and descriptions he has Prometheus cry out (1080): *kai mên ergôi kouketi muthôi* (yes, in fact, and no longer merely in word); i.e., this time it is the real earthquake, no mere talk. See note on 245.

848–860 The division of the Chorus may have begun during this epode-like addition to 832–47; typical divisions of the lines are given by OCT[2] and Rose, p. 232.

The combination of *autodêla* (self-evident) and *autophona* (self-slain), with *dipla, diduma* (twofold) and *dimoira* (doubly-fated) in these lines synthesizes the common destiny of the brothers.

What to call this? what but sorrows
born of sorrows bred in the home?
Come, my friends, as sounds of woe stir the air,
smite your heads, your hands falling with a
rhythmic stroke, 855

852–853 *sorrows born of sorrows:* cf. 740–41. The phrase sounds almost like a proverbial quotation; it suggests the chainlike process that is developed in the *Oresteia.*

853 *bred in the home:* in Greek, "settled on the hearth"; the phrase recalls in ironic fashion the words used by ETEOCLES in 73, "established homes" (homes with hearths).

854–860 The clue to this passage lies in the word *theôrida* (sacred vessel) 857, the ship with a sacred mission to Apollo on Delos so familiar from its association with the postponement of Socrates' execution: "This is the ship, according to the Athenians, in which Theseus went to Crete with the fourteen young men and women, and saved them and himself [from the Minotaur]. Now the Athenians had vowed to Apollo that if the young people were saved they would send a sacred mission to Delos every year. So, from that time to the present day they have continued to send the mission to the god. Now, once the mission has been started, according to the law no one must be publicly executed" (Plato, *Phaedo* 58A-B). The pervading nautical metaphor is developed in a different sense here, following the pattern set in 689–90. The voyage is completely contrasted with the sacred journey to Delos, and is best portrayed in schematic form:

Need for a favorable breeze.	Mourners' sighs.
Oars.	Beating of mourners' hands.
Crossing the sea.	Crossing the Acheron.
Garlands, white sails.	No fancy rigging, black sails.
Accessible to Apollo.	Not touched by Apollo.
Sailed, presumably, in daylight.	Never saw the sun.
Sent to Delos(the*visible* land).	Never saw the sun.

But in each case there is hospitality.

855 *smite . . . rhythmic:* in Greek, *eressete* (row, ply oars); the same verb is used in the lament in *The Persians* 1046, *eress', eresse,* and it is echoed in 1054 by *arasse* (smite).

as with the plashing stroke that speeds over
the Acheron,
constantly, the sacred vessel with its unblest
sails of black,
where Apollo never sets foot, no sunlight falls,
to a land open to all, but unseen. 860

[Here now, to perform a bitter task, come
Antigone and Ismene, sisters
to lament brothers. Heartfelt is their grief;
I know that from the depths of their lovely
bosoms will rise a fitting song of woe. 865

---

856 *Acheron:* a river of the Underworld. See note on 690.

857 I read *astolon* instead of OCT[2]'s *astonon,* i.e., ([voyage] that is no voyage) instead of ([voyage] full of lament), and omit *naustolon* (voyage) as a gloss on *theôrida* (see note on 854).

860 *open to all:* this term befits Delos, center of Apollo's worship (see *Homeric Hymn to Apollo* 56–60): "all men will bring hecatombs and gather here . . ."); but no one is more hospitable, open to all (*pandokon* in this line) than the God of the Underworld (see *Homeric Hymn to Demeter* 9, where he is called Polydectes, Host to many, or, in a variant form, Polydegmon [404 and 430], and Aeschylus, *The Suppliants* 157, *poluxenôtatos* [most hospitable]). We recall the *pandokeutria* (all welcoming) Mother Earth, above, in line 18, who will later welcome her children in death.

It should be noted that the phrases "where Apollo never sets foot, no sunlight falls" might apply both to the ship and to the land.

861–874 If any lines in this play could reasonably be called inferior they form this passage. The choral lament that begins in 875 would most appropriately follow 860 without interruption. Many editors feel—I think rightly—that this passage was inserted to introduce the sisters (cf. Introduction, pages 23–24), hitherto quite unnecessary, to whom are ascribed some parts of the following lament. It may well be that as some suggest, the interpolator had at his disposal two good soloists, whom he made full use of in the ending of the play. The present passage is little more than stage directions and exposition.

863–865 The sincerity of the newcomers' grief matches that of the CHORUS (873–74).

But, before their lament, it falls to us
to raise the discordant hymn of the Fury
and sing for Hades
the hateful paean of triumph. 870
Alas!
Most unhappy in your brothers of all those
who wear the neatly girt robes of women,
I weep and wail aloud; and none can doubt
that my cries come truly from the heart.]

The CHORUS divides into two groups.

STROPHE 1

FIRST SEMICHORUS *Alas, misguided ones!* 875

866–870 This presumably refers to 875–960, in particular 951–60; for a paean of the Erinyes, cf. *Agamemnon* 645, *The Libation Bearers* 150–51, *The Eumenides* 331.

872 An impossible line. "Not a very happy line," says Rose. It is a poor attempt to reproduce passages like 927–28, where the relative clause says something significant.

875 A lament begins here, which, I think, in the original play must have continued to the end without such interruptions as 1005–53, but not necessarily in the form of the preserved text. For a valuable account of such laments, see H. D. Broadhead's *Persae*, pages 310–17. Lines 875–960 have some characteristics of the ritual lament (for instance, verbal repetition), but serve rather as a reflective stasimon introducing the lament proper. In the preserved text they must be regarded as a third stasimon; in the original, as I see it, they actually began the exodus, which continued with theatrical ritual as the CHORUS moved out chanting its antiphonal lament.

Murray in OCT[2] attributes part of the stasimon to ANTIGONE and ISMENE *dubitanter*; the translation follows suggestions of ascription made by Lloyd-Jones, and assigns these lyrics to the CHORUS only. The CHORUS divides into semichoruses, but occasionally sings in unison. Later, one semichorus clearly refers to Polynices, the other to ETEOCLES; this division corresponds to the sympathies of ANTIGONE and ISMENE, if they are present.

The CHORUS notes that the two brothers have fulfilled Oedipus' curse, bringing disaster to themselves and to their family and to the city. Their warlike feud gained them property—a burial lot

you heeded no friends, sufferings did not deter you;
you ruined your father's house,
unhappy ones, with force!

FULL CHORUS *Unhappy, yes! and unhappy were the deaths*
they found in their assault on the house! 880

ANTISTROPHE 1

SECOND SEMICHORUS *Alas, you that brought low*
your family, and fixed your eyes on a bitter
sovereignty! Now your quarrel
is settled—by the sword. 885

FULL CHORUS *Too truly, roused by their father, Oedipus,*
the mighty Fury won fulfillment.

STROPHE 2

FIRST SEMICHORUS *Their wounds were on the left side; the*
wounds

—and brought troubles both for the city and for its foes; their mother is especially singled out as a woman of misfortune. The concluding strophe and antistrophe concentrate the metaphorical aspects of these autochthonous blood-brothers and celebrate the total triumph of the Fury-Curses: the wind of Destiny has not merely changed (cf. 705–8); it has ended, calmed down (960).

875–878 Although the brothers are addressed as a pair, the adjectival phrases suggest some distinction between ETEOCLES and Polynices; in 877–78 we read *domous helontes patrôious* (having destroyed your father's home) in 883–84 *pikrâs monarkhiâs idontes* (having seen bitter sovereignty); the former phrase fits Polynices, the latter ETEOCLES.

876 *heeded no friends:* another reference to the impetuousness that apparently characterized the family of Laius.

878 *unhappy:* repeated in 879, repetition being natural in the formal lament; see 888 (wounds), 892–93 (alas!), 904–5 (goods), 911–12 (smitten).

884–885 Cf. Introduction, pages 16–18, and also 933–37. The word *epekrânen* (won fulfillment), last word in the next sentence (887), suggests that the matter is finished.

888 *left side:* E. A. Havelock has suggested to me the following interpretation of this passage: they fought face to face; each dropped his shield and sprang, striking with his right hand against the

went through the ribs of men born
of the same mother; they pierced 890
[clear to the very heart.]
Alas, demented men!
Alas, the curse, where death
demanded requital!

FULL CHORUS *A deep, deadly blow you speak of, heavy* 895
on the house and its people,
from the terrible might
of a father's curse that
brought them unanimous doom.

ANTISTROPHE 2

SECOND SEMICHORUS *Throughout the city, too, goes lament;* 900
our bulwarks lament; and the ground
that loves her sons laments; but
their goods await followers—
goods which led them to doom,
goods, which brought about strife 905
and brought an end in death.

FULL CHORUS *They divided their goods in bitter wrath*
and each got his equal share;
but the arbiter won

---

other's left; hence the stress on the mutuality and symmetry of their wounds. Cf. 899.

891 A line has been lost in the manuscript.

899 *unanimous:* see 811–12 and 888.

900–902 *lament, lament, laments: stenos, stenousi, stenei*; a repetitive sequence, the latter form of which rhymes with *menei* (await) at the end of 902; see also *epigonois* (followers) and *ainomorois* (led to doom) at the ends of 903 and 904, and *sidêroplêktoi . . . ekhousin* (smitten they lie) and *sidêroplêktoi . . . menousi* (smitten they wait) in 911–12.

901*ff* An obvious reminiscence of the Sown Men legend.

903 This line is taken by some to show that Aeschylus referred to a second attack by the *Epigonoi* (the second generation). But Aeschylus, if obscure, was not a careless artist, and he specifically calls ETEOCLES and Polynices childless in 828. Cf. Introduction, page 24 and footnote 48.

905– The property led to a bloody division and the arbiter was the God

angry blame from their friends
and no joy came from their strife. 910

STROPHE 3

FIRST SEMICHORUS *Smitten by the sword they lie before us,*
smitten by the sword they lie awaiting—
waiting for what? one might ask;
burial in their father's lot.

SECOND SEMICHORUS *They have from us loud-ringing cries as escort,* 915
a heart-rending lament,
soulful in grief and anguish,
passionate, with no thought of joy,
amid tears that flow from a heart
that truly seems to be breaking 920
as I weep for
these two princes lying here.

ANTISTROPHE 3

FIRST SEMICHORUS *This, one may say over these hapless men:*
much have they done to their own countrymen
and to all hostile forces,
and many died in battle. 925

---

910 of War; disastrous strife and the God of Strife bracket the picture of the division.

911–912 The last word in the preceding stanza is *Ares,* who wielded the sword that we have heard so much of since 727–30; the next stanza begins with *sidêroplêktoi,* which is repeated at the start of 912. The brothers are clearly treated alike, as the parallelism of the lines shows (cf. also 908); there is no need for controversy.

914 *burial . . . lot:* the Greek uses *lakhai,* a word which apparently may mean either "diggings" or "allotments." Cf. Introduction, page 17 and footnote 34. See also 1002–3.

915 A corrupt line with no satisfactory emendation. For the picture, see the last line of *The Persians* (1077), where Xerxes leaves the stage with none of the brilliant escort with which he started: "I shall escort you with woeful laments," says the Chorus.

916–917 Repetition of sounds here in *daïktêr goos autostonos autopêmôn daïophrôn.*

922– What might have been a eulogy of dead patriots is here con-

SECOND SEMICHORUS *Wretched was the mother who bore them, wretched*
beyond all who are hailed
as the bearers of children;
it was her own son whom she took
as husband, and she bore these men,
who died as we see, each brother 930
slain by the hand
of brother of the same seed.

STROPHE 4

FIRST SEMICHORUS *Of the same seed, yes, now utterly destroyed,*
in no friendly partition,
in a maddened rivalry; 935
and so their strife was ended.

FULL CHORUS *Ended now their hatred; in the earth*
drenched with blood their life lies
mingled; now they truly share their blood. 940
Bitter the arbiter of strife, a stranger

---

925 verted into a comment on the disastrous results of the brothers' feud. As before, we see that they are linked closely with the community in their destiny.

926–932 Grief for the mother almost inevitably arouses reminiscence of the Sown Men and their fratricidal strife. The close link between the two enemies is marked by the use of *homosporois* (of the same seed) as the last word in the third antistrophe (932) followed by *homosporoi*, first word in the fourth strophe (933). This blood-link between them is strongly contrasted with the violence of their dispute, which needed death to end it; so we find 936 ending *en teleutâi* (at the end) and 937 begins *pepautai d' ekhthos* (finished is the hatred).

933 *utterly destroyed:* this implies that the whole family is destroyed; see Introduction, pages 24–25, and note on 884.

938–946 Here we have a piling up of the words and images that have been so prominent as we moved to a climax: earth drenched with mingled blood, blood kinship, the steel arbiter of the father's estate, the allotment of earth.

941 *bitter:* repeated in 944 and recalling the "bitter sovereignty" of 883–84.

fire-forged, sped from overseas,
whetted steel! Bitter, though fair, the divider
of their goods, Ares, by whom the father's curse 945
was brought to fulfillment.

ANTISTROPHE 4

SECOND SEMICHORUS *They hold the lot which they won, unhappy men,*
of apportionments sent by god,
and beneath their bodies earth's
wealth will stretch unlimited. 950

FULL CHORUS *Alas, with many wreaths of sorrow*
you crowned your family!
Now at the last a cry has been raised

941–942 *a stranger . . . from overseas:* a characteristic Aeschylean word-play, referring to the forged steel that killed the brothers; the Chalybes, workers in iron (728), were associated with the Pontus, the Black Sea, and are therefore doubly called *pontios* (from overseas) and *Pontic;* moreover, the Black Sea, because of its stormy reputation, was apotropaically called *Euxeinos,* the Euxine, or "hospitable" sea, which adds point to *xeinos* (stranger-friend).

946 A good final effect in this strophe is achieved by the last two words, *titheis alêthê* (rendering true).

947–948 Another ironic reference to the theme of lots, chance, in contrast with careful planning. The Greek text helps to make the picture vivid: *ekhousi moiran lakhontes hoi meleoi diodotôn laxeôn* (they hold a portion which they got, poor wretches, of god-given allotments)—poor wretches surrounded by allotments beyond their control.

949–950 More irony; a mere six-foot lot on the surface, but it stretches immeasurably below. The word *ploutos* (wealth) evokes other connotations.

951–960 The climax, the paean of the Furies.
wreaths of sorrow: the athletic victors' wreaths were the result of *ponoi* (struggles) here "sorrows" as in 740 and 852–53.

952 *crowned:* literally, put a top crown on," another hint of the finality of the process. The first word in the next sentence (953) is

by the Curses—a shrill strain sung at the rout
of the house in utter flight; 955
and Sinful Folly's trophy stands at the gate
where these men died; in triumph over these two
the Fury found its end. 960

FIRST SEMICHORUS *You struck and were stricken.*

SECOND SEMICHORUS *You killed and were killed.*

FIRST SEMICHORUS *With the spear you killed.*

SECOND SEMICHORUS *By the spear you died.*

FIRST SEMICHORUS *Wretched in doing—*

SECOND SEMICHORUS *Wretched in suffering—*

---

teleutaiai (last, final) not merely *teleiai* (fulfilling).

954–955 Literally, "the family having been turned in completely routing flight"; could anything be more specific? It is all over with the family.

956 The gates of the city mark, not only the point where the Argives were turned back, but also the point where the struggle between Apollo's anger, Oedipus' curse, and the Furies, with the family of Laius came to an end. Triumph over *these two* caused the evil wind of destiny to drop (*elêxe daimôn,* the last two words of the ode; see notes on 705 and 875).

It is perhaps important to note the point of the *tropaion,* the symbol of rout—namely, the gates; the gates have held, the city is safe.

961–1004 A similar lament with ritualistic repetition and antiphony ends Aeschylus' *The Persians*. The distribution of lines here is somewhat uncertain, especially if ANTIGONE and ISMENE are introduced; in the translation I have attributed the lines to SEMICHORUSES and the full CHORUS. The lament consists largely of antiphonal utterances in pairs that together form one metrical line; the meter may be classed as free lyric iambics, but there are three double dochmiacs in 971, 982, and 995–97; the first two are parallel in meaning—one brother killed the other; the third notes how the events affected the household, the land, and the people. In general, the FIRST SEMICHORUS ("ANTIGONE") laments over Polynices, the

FIRST SEMICHORUS *Let lament rise!*

SECOND SEMICHORUS *Let the tears flow!*

FIRST SEMICHORUS *You lie dead.* 965

SECOND SEMICHORUS *You that killed.*

STROPHE

FIRST SEMICHORUS *Alas!*

SECOND SEMICHORUS *Alas!*

FIRST SEMICHORUS *My mind is maddened with grief.*

SECOND SEMICHORUS *Within me my heart is groaning.*

FIRST SEMICHORUS *In grief for you, pitiful one.*

SECOND SEMICHORUS *And you, too, utterly wretched.* 970

FIRST SEMICHORUS *By your kin you were slain.*

SECOND SEMICHORUS *And you slew your own kin.*

FIRST SEMICHORUS *Twofold to speak of—*

SECOND SEMICHORUS *Twofold to look on—*

FIRST SEMICHORUS *Here we see your griefs before us.*

SECOND SEMICHORUS *Yes, brother-anguish, side by side.*

FULL CHORUS *Destiny, grievous bestower of heavy ills,* 975
O awesome shade of Oedipus,
black Spirit of Vengeance, how mighty is your power!

SECOND ("ISMENE") over ETEOCLES, but there are apparently exceptions, as in 973–74 and 984–85.

964 Parenthetical; line 963 continues in 965.

971 *your kin, your own kin:* in Greek *philou, philon.*

973–974 Here and in the corresponding 984–85 one can do little more than guess at the text and meaning.

975–977 The carefully patterned antiphonal lament of 961–74 is given added weight by the refrain of the CHORUS (repeated in 986–88),

ANTISTROPHE

SECOND SEMICHORUS *Alas!*

FIRST SEMICHORUS *Alas!*

SECOND SEMICHORUS *Sufferings hard to behold—*

FIRST SEMICHORUS *You brought, returned from exile.*

SECOND SEMICHORUS *This one came not home, though he killed.* 980

FIRST SEMICHORUS *This one came home, but lost his life.*

SECOND SEMICHORUS *Yes, one brother was slain* 982

FIRST SEMICHORUS *as he killed his brother.*

SECOND SEMICHORUS *Dreadful to speak of—* 993

FIRST SEMICHORUS *Dreadful to look on—*

SECOND SEMICHORUS *Mournful sorrows of men akin.* 984

FIRST SEMICHORUS *Tearful sufferings, wave on wave.* 985

FULL CHORUS *Destiny, grievous bestower of heavy ills,*
O awesome shade of Oedipus,

---

which concentrates in three lines the power of Destiny, the threat of the dead Oedipus, and the power of the curse evoked by Oedipus.

978 I assume that here the SECOND SEMICHORUS ("ISMENE") begins the stanza, in contrast with the order in the strophe (967). Lines 978 and 980 refer to ETEOCLES, 979 and 981 to Polynices.

980 *came not home:* from battle.

981 *came home:* from exile.

984 *homônuma* (of the same name) at the end of the line in the OCT[2] is taken by some to refer to Polynices' name "man of much strife"; Rose suggests that it is an intrusive gloss on another word in the line, *kêde(a)*, which can mean both "relationship" and "grief" (cf. *Agamemnon* 699–700, where Helen is a *kêdos,* a bride and a disaster to Troy). I have translated an emendation, by Weil, *homaimona* (of kindred blood).

985 *wave on wave:* represents in this corrupt passage some form of *tripaltos* (triply shaken) or simply (triple); Rose speaks of a triple

black Spirit of Vengeance, how mighty is your power!

FIRST SEMICHORUS *This power you know, for you felt it—*

SECOND SEMICHORUS *You, too, learned it at the same time—* 990

FIRST SEMICHORUS *When you returned to the city.*

SECOND SEMICHORUS *When your spear threatened your brother.* 992

FIRST SEMICHORUS *Unhappy race!* 983

SECOND SEMICHORUS *Unhappy fate!*

FIRST SEMICHORUS *Alas, what pain!* 994

SECOND SEMICHORUS *Alas, what wrongs!*

FIRST SEMICHORUS *To the house and the land* 995
[Above all to me.]

SECOND SEMICHORUS *And even more, to me.*

---

onset. The word certainly recalls the triple warning of Apollo, the three generations, and the triple-crested waves (760).

989 Lines 989 and 991 refer to Polynices, 990 and 992 to ETEOCLES.
you felt it: i.e., the Fury, mentioned in 986–88. The phrase is somewhat obscure and has been variously interpreted; among the suggestions are "you crossed [from the Peloponnesus]," "you crossed [the Acheron]," "you pierced him."

991 *returned:* in Greek, *katêlthes,* often used of a returning exile.

992 *threatened:* the Greek has *antêretâs* (counter-oarsman) used above in 282–83 and 595 for Cadmeian champions; combination of this with *katêlthes* above makes reference to Polynices in 991 and ETEOCLES ("your brother") in 992 unavoidable.

995 Hermann suggested that this line should be divided; the suggestion is accepted in the OCT[2]. My translation treats the line as a single utterance by the FIRST SEMICHORUS, followed by 997 uttered by the SECOND SEMICHORUS; I suggest that 996 is a gloss on 997. With such a scheme, we have two divided iambic trimeters (983, 994) followed by two undivided dochmiacs—eminently satisfactory if, as Lloyd-Jones suggests, symmetry is desirable. The phrase *to prosô* (997), which has disturbed modern editors (Rose suggests "in the future"), may also have prompted annotation by some ancient scholar.

FIRST SEMICHORUS *Alas, for your grievous sorrows, my prince*

• • • • • •

SECOND SEMICHORUS . . .
Eteocles, my commander.

FIRST SEMICHORUS *Alas, these two, most wretched of all men!* 1000

SECOND SEMICHORUS *In foolish sin infatuate!*

FIRST SEMICHORUS *In what ground shall we lay their bodies?*

SECOND SEMICHORUS *Wherever the honor is greatest.*

FULL CHORUS *Alas, what grief, to lie by their father's side!*

A HERALD enters.

998–999 It is generally assumed that there is a lacuna in this area, two lines being lost that refer to Polynices and match the reference to ETEOCLES in 998–99. I suggest that the couplet referring to Polynices preceded reference to ETEOCLES, following the symmetrical pattern that I have assumed already in eliminating 996 as a gloss on 997; and the fact that 999 was almost lost in the manuscript tradition (see OCT²'s apparatus) makes it possible that the lacuna lies between 998 and 999, not after 999. As the translation stands, the pattern of alternate speeches by "ANTIGONE" and "ISMENE," i.e., the FIRST and SECOND SEMICHORUSES, remains consistent from 989 to 1003.

1000 In Greek an effective example of alliteration: *pantôn poluponôtatô.*

1001 Literally, "demon-possessed"; for the *daimôn,* see 705 and 960.

1002–1003 *what ground . . . honor is greatest:* another recollection of the Sown Men; they will be buried with their parents and relatives.

1004 A closing line, which along with ironic comment on 1003 adds impressive alliteration to sinister ambiguity; *pêma patri pareunon* (misery lying beside a father)—sinister, whatever we regard as the implications of *pêma;* Oedipus, Laius, the mother-wife, ETEOCLES, and Polynices are all involved.

[HERALD I must report the will and decision 1005
of the state council of Cadmus' city:
Eteocles here, loyal to his land,
shall be buried in his own land's embrace;
he chose death, his town's bulwark against foes;
pure and blameless in what his fathers revered, 1010
he died where death is noble for the young.

1005 *Exit scene,* to 1078. On 1005–53, which, like many others, I regard as interpolated, see Introduction, pages 22–25. It cannot, I must repeat, be cut out purely on stylistic grounds, though occasionally lines like 1011 suggest the cliché or pastiche.

1006 *state council:* in Greek, *probouloi* (of the *dêmos*), i.e., provisional state advisers in a time of emergency. The idea that this phrase, recalling the Athenian *probouloi* of 412 B.C., is proof of the lateness of the passage has been demolished, along with other faulty objections, by Lloyd-Jones; it has no bearing on my own views of the spuriousness of the lines. Rose aptly describes some of the passage as "a good and spirited paraphrase of Sophocles."

1007 *loyal:* translates OCT²'s *eunoiâi* (good will). (This is a correction of the Medicean manuscript's *eunaiâi,* the equivalent of *eunêi* (bed, or lying). The translated reading is commonplace; the other reading seems to involve a good Aeschylean metaphor related to the mother-earth and similar pictures in the play; the picture may, in fact, be continued in 1008 with the word *philais* (loving, and one's own).

1009 *bulwark:* translation of an almost certainly correct emendation, by Wakefield, *stegôn* (warding off); for the use of this verb in connection with the city walls, see 216, 234, and 797.

1010 Here ETEOCLES differed from Oedipus, who violated his father's rights.

1011 This line recalls a patriotic exhortation of the Spartans by Tyrtaeus in frags. 6 and 7 Diehl: frag. 6 begins, "Lying dead is a noble thing if one has fallen in the front line of battle"; the poet then urges the younger Spartans to fight bravely, noting that "it is scandalous to find older men killed in the front line" (frag. 7. 21–22), but that "for younger men everything [of that sort] is appropriate" (7. 27). Tyrtaeus' passage is derived from Homer, *The Iliad* 22. 66–76, where Priam contrasts the horror of an old man's death at the hands of an invading enemy with the glory of a young hero's death.

So it is decreed for Eteocles.
But his brother, dead Polynices here,
cast him forth unburied, a prey for dogs;
for he would have uprooted Cadmus' land, 1015
had not some god blocked him, through his brother,
this hero; though dead he will bear the curse
of his father's gods, whom he dishonored,
attacking this town with an alien force.
This, too: the wide-winged birds shall bury him 1020
in dishonor, a fit reward for him;
no hands shall scatter earth over his corpse,
there shall be no service of shrill lament,
no honor of funeral given by his friends.
So has decreed our Cadmeian council. 1025

ANTIGONE What Cadmeian council? I tell them this:
though no one else help me, I shall bury
Polynices myself, facing the risk
involved; he's my brother; I feel no shame
in defying lawless authority. 1030
Awesome is that single womb we came from,

1016 *some god . . . through his brother:* almost as noncommittal and practical as some of ETEOCLES' utterances.

1017–1019 The civic pronouncement is at variance with the idea that the family hatred has ended with the deaths of the two princes; what we have here is the view of Creon in Sophocles' *Antigone;* from this viewpoint death does not cancel all debts.

1020 *winged birds:* his body will be the prey of carrion birds as well as dogs (1014); ANTIGONE adds another possibility to be rejected in 1035. The use of "winged" is more than ornamental; it suggests the larger birds with wider wingspread.

1026 *What Cadmeian council?*: a free translation in an effort to reproduce the indignant scorn of ANTIGONE; she begins with a proud *egô*, then says *Kadmeiôn ge*, where *ge* is almost a snort of derision—the old-fashioned *forsooth!*

1029–1030 Perhaps ambiguous: (a) I am not ashamed to regard this unconstitutional civic group as unworthy of obedience; or (b) I am not ashamed to show such disobedient lawlessness toward the city.

1031 Cf. *Prometheus Bound* 39: "kinship, you know, is an awesome thing. . . ." What is a commonplace statement in *Prometheus* is much more significant here.

a mother wretched, an ill-starred begetter.
So I who live must share with the dead one
grief unwanted, showing a sister's love.
His flesh no hollow-bellied wolves, either, 1035
shall feed on; let none make me this decree!
Earth to cover him in burial rites
I myself, a mere woman, will provide,
bringing it in my folded linen robes;
I will cover him! None shall decree me! No! 1040

1033–1034 A troublesome forced antithesis, literally: "therefore, willing with one unwilling, O my soul, share sorrows with a dead one while living, with a kindred mind." I have turned the self-exhortation into a firm statement.

1035 This line is often split on the assumption that there is a lacuna between the first and second parts, including a second reference to dogs and birds (see 1014 and 1020). I suspect that this assumption is unnecessary; the dogs and birds having already been mentioned, ANTIGONE adds, "the wolves won't get him, either," or "not even the wolves will get him."

1036 She speaks in the tone of 1026; see also 1040.

1037–1040 ANTIGONE repeats her intentions emphatically but not clearly, thanks to line 1039. It is not likely that she plans personally to dig a grave for Polynices and bury him or personally to cremate him and bury his ashes; it is more likely that she thinks personally in terms of a symbolic burial like that of Sophocles' *Antigone*. For this she would need some soil and, at least, water, and she might well contrive to carry this in the folds of her robe. But the Greek text does not say so: in line 1039 ANTIGONE says, "In the folds of my robe carrying . . ."—carrying what? No object is given. One might by a kind of metonymy extort something like "burial materials" out of the nouns in line 1037. It is just possible that line 1039 is corrupt; if *peplômatos* were a gloss to indicate the kind of robe that would have a pocket-fold, one could insert something like *gên hudôr te* (earth and water) in the middle of the line. Unfortunately we must apparently admit that we have here a clumsy reminiscence of Sophocles. The translation assumes that ANTIGONE will carry earth with her on her planned trip to "bury" Polynices.

I have the will, the means will not fail me.

HERALD I bid you defy not the city thus.

ANTIGONE And I bid you waste no edicts on me.

HERALD A town just saved from ruin is harsh, you know.

ANTIGONE True; yet this man shall not lie unburied. 1045

HERALD You think your city's foe deserves a tomb?

ANTIGONE The gods set what he deserves some time ago.

HERALD No, not till he imperiled his own land!

ANTIGONE He suffered ill; so he repayed ill with ill.

HERALD But he struck at all to avenge one man. 1050

ANTIGONE Dispute—even among gods—wants the last word.

HERALD Well, be self-willed! I prohibit burial.

ANTIGONE And I shall bury him. Waste no more words!]

The HERALD leaves.

1042–1053 This line-by-line interchange is marked at the beginning by ANTIGONE picking up the HERALD's words: *audô* (1042), *audô* (1043); *trâkhus ge* (1044), *trâkhûn'* (1045).

1047 A difficult line. Again ANTIGONE picks up one of the HERALD's words (*tîmêseis*, 1046, and *diatetîmêtai*, 1047); she seems to think that what is due Polynices has been assessed once and for all; he was her brother. But the HERALD insists that Polynices' unpatriotic action decided the issue.

1049–1050 When ANTIGONE appeals to a familiar code of behavior—good for good, evil for evil—the HERALD points out that Polynices went too far in his vengeance.

1051 ANTIGONE is getting nowhere, and says, "Arguments can go on forever."

1052–1053 I have adopted Paley's suggestion that 1052 and 1053 be transposed; thus we need assume no lacuna after 1050 (as indicated in Murray's OCT[2]).

self-willed—she is a worthy member of the family of Laius. Cf. Sophocles, *Antigone* 471–72: "here there can be seen the harsh breeding derived from a harsh father in the daughter."

CHORUS *Alas!*
You may now boast loudly, ruin of the house,
vengeful Spirits of Doom, who have thus destroyed 1055
the family of Oedipus, root and branch.

LEADER OF SECOND SEMICHORUS *What must I feel? or do? what course must I take?*
How can I refuse to bewail you?
or refuse an escort to your tomb?
But I fear and shrink in terror before 1060
the city's dread power.

LEADER OF FIRST SEMICHORUS *You at least will find many mourners;*
but that one, hapless and unlamented,
has only his sister's wails to escort him
to his tomb. Who can approve of that? 1065

FIRST SEMICHORUS *Whether the city punish or not*
those who bewail Polynices,
we shall go forth and help to bury him,
escorting him thus; for the whole household
shares this grief, and a city may change views 1070
on what it commends as right and just.

1054–1078 In these final anapests I follow the ascriptions suggested by Lloyd-Jones.

1056 *root and branch:* see 71 and Introduction, page 24.

1057–1061 The speaker, like Ismene in Sophocles' play, has not the courage to defy authority, whereas the next speaker ends on a defiant note unlike the timid ending of the former speaker.

1062–1063 This recalls what ETEOCLES himself said would happen to a leader who failed (6–8).

1066–1071 The SEMICHORUS echoes the defiant tone of the preceding speaker but concludes with a sophistic relativism (1070–71) that seems more Sophoclean than Aeschylean and can hardly be regarded as characteristic of the choral group we have hitherto seen.

1069–1071 As far as the family is concerned, dissension is ended, whatever the prevailing civic view may be.

SECOND SEMICHORUS *But we go with this man, as the city,*
besides what is right and just, commends;
for, next to the Blessed Ones and mighty Zeus,
this man rescued the Cadmeians' city, 1075
and it did not capsize beneath a flood
of alien foes,
overwhelmed in utter disaster.

The divided CHORUS leaves, the FIRST SEMICHORUS escorting the body of POLYNICES, the SECOND that of ETEOCLES.

1072–1078 The other SEMICHORUS associates the city's present view with what is right and justifies its devotion to ETEOCLES by a fitting tribute to his heroic defense of the city.

1076*ff* A magnificent recurrence of the nautical metaphor.

1078 *in utter disaster*: the last words of the play *ta malista* (most of all, utterly); they have been objected to by editors, who tend to refer them primarily to "rescued" in 1075; but the phrase belongs obviously to the preceding word, "overwhelmed," and reflects the thought that although the prince perished, the city survived.

BIBLIOGRAPHY

Useful texts and commentaries

Broadhead, H. D., *The Persae of Aeschylus*. Cambridge: Cambridge University Press, 1960.

Mazon, P., *Eschyle* (Budé edition). Paris: Société d' édition "Les belles lettres," 1920–25.

Murray, G., *Aeschyli Septem Quae Supersunt Tragoediae*, 2nd ed. Oxford: The Clarendon Press, 1955 (referred to as OCT²). In a few cases readings from the first edition (Oxford: The Clarendon Press, 1937) have been preferred to those of the second.

Paley, F. A., *The Tragedies of Aeschylus*, 3rd ed. London: Bibliotheca Classica, eds. George Long and A. J. Macleane, 1870.

Rose, H. J., *A Commentary on the Surviving Plays of Aeschylus*, vol. 1. Amsterdam: Noord-Hollandsche Uitg. Mij., 1957.

Smyth, H. W., *Aeschylus* (The Loeb Classical Library), 2 vols. Cambridge, Mass.: Harvard University Press; London: William Heinemann Ltd., 1952.

Tucker, T. G., *"The Seven Against Thebes" of Aeschylus*. Cambridge: Cambridge University Press, 1908.

Verrall, A. W., *"The Seven Against Thebes" of Aeschylus*. London: Macmillan & Co. Ltd., 1887.

Wilamowitz-Moellendorf, U. von, *Aeschyli tragoediae*. Berlin: Weidmann, 1914.

Selected articles relevant to the play

Cameron, H. D., "The Debt to Earth in the *Seven Against Thebes*," *Transactions of the American Philological Association*, 95 (1964), 1–8.

Dawe, R. D., "Inconsistencies of Plot and Character in Aeschylus," *Proceedings of the Cambridge Philological Society*, 189 (1963), 21–62.

———, "The End of *Seven Against Thebes,*" *The Classical Quarterly,* n.s., 17 (1967), 16–28.

Dawson, Christopher M., "The Dark Shadow of Oedipus," *Annual Bulletin of the Classical Association of New England,* 57 (1962), 10–11 (abstract).

Finley, John H., Jr., "The *Septem:* The Hero and the Polis," *Annual Bulletin of the Classical Association of New England,* 57 (1962), 12 (abstract).

Fraenkel, E., "Die sieben Redepaare in Thebaner Drama des Aischylos," *Sitzungsb. Bayer. Akad.,* 1957, Heft 5.

———, "Zum Schluss der Sieben gegen Theben," *Museum Helveticum,* 21 (1964), 58–64.

Fritz, Kurt von, "Die Gestalt des Eteokles in Aischylos' *Sieben gegen Theben,*" pp. 193–226 in his *Antike und moderne Tragödie,* Berlin: W. de Gruyter, 1962.

Howe, Thalia Phillies, "Suicide and Self-Slaying in the *Septem,*" *Annual Bulletin of the Classical Association of New England,* 57 (1962), 11 (abstract).

———, "Taboo in the Oedipus Theme," *Transactions of the American Philological Association,* 93 (1962), 124–43 (especially 130–33).

Kitto, H. D. F., "The Idea of God in Aeschylus and Sophocles," *La Notion du divin depuis Homère à Platon* (Fondation Hardt: Entretiens 1), Geneva: Vandoeuvres, 1952, 165–89.

Lesky, A., "Eteokles in den Sieben gegen Theben," *Wiener Studien,* 74 (1961), 5–17.

Lloyd-Jones, H., "The End of the *Seven Against Thebes,*" *The Classical Quarterly,* n.s., 9 (1959), 80–115.

Otis, B., "The Unity of the *Seven Against Thebes,*" *Greek, Roman, and Byzantine Studies,* 3 (1960), 153–74.

Patzer, H., "Die dramatische Handlung der *Sieben gegen Theben,*" *Harvard Studies in Classical Philology,* 63 (1958), 97–119.

Podlecki, Anthony J., "The Character of Eteocles in Aeschylus' *Septem,*" *Transactions of the American Philological Association,* 95 (1964), 283–99.

Rosenmeyer, Thomas, "Seven Against Thebes: The Tragedy of War," *Arion,* 1 (1962), 48–78.

Schadewaldt, W., "Die Wappnung des Eteokles: Zu Aischylos *Sieben gegen Theben,*" *Eranion (Festschrift für H. Hommel),* Tübingen: M. Niemeyer, 1961, 105–16.

Snell, B., "Septem," pp. 78–95 in his *Aischylos und das Handeln im Drama (Philologus, Supplementband,* 20, 1).

Solmsen, F., "The Erinys in Aischylos' *Septem,*" *Transactions of the American Philological Association,* 68 (1937), 197–211.

Wolff, E., "Die Entscheidung des Eteokles in den *Sieben gegen Theben,*" *Harvard Studies in Classical Philology,* 63 (1958), 89–95.

BIBLIOGRAPHY

Books discussing Greek drama in general and Aeschylus in particular

Dumortier, Jean, *Les Images dans la poésie d'Eschyle*. Paris: Société d'édition "Les belles lettres," 1933.

Earp, F. E., *The Style of Aeschylus*. Cambridge: Cambridge University Press, 1948.

Finley, John H., Jr., *Pindar and Aeschylus*. Cambridge, Mass.: Harvard University Press, 1955.

Golden, Leon, *In Praise of Prometheus*. Chapel Hill: University of North Carolina Press, 1966.

Harsh, Philip W., *A Handbook of Classical Drama*. Stanford: Stanford University Press, 1963.

Kitto, H. D. F., *Greek Tragedy: A Literary Study*. London: 1950; New York: Doubleday Anchor, 1954.

Lesky, A., *Greek Tragedy*, trans. H. A. Frankfort. London: E. Benn; New York: Barnes & Noble, Inc., 1965.

Murray, G., *Aeschylus, the Creator of Tragedy*. Oxford: The Clarendon Press, 1964.

Norwood, G., *Greek Tragedy*, 4th ed. London: Methuen & Co. Ltd., 1953.

Owen, E. T., *The Harmony of Aeschylus*. Toronto: Clarke, Irwin, 1952.

Pohlenz, Max, *Die griechische Tragödie*, 2nd ed. Göttingen: Vanderhoeck & Ruprecht, 1954.

Sheppard, J. T., *Greek Tragedy*. Cambridge: Cambridge University Press, 1934.

Smyth, H. W., *Aeschylean Tragedy*. Berkeley: University of California Press, 1924.

Stanford, W. B., *Aeschylus in His Style*. Dublin: The University Press, 1942.

Wilamowitz-Moellendorf, U. von, *Aischylos: Interpretationen*. Berlin: Weidmann, 1914.

Other works cited

Diehl, E., *Anthologia lyrica graeca*, vol. 1, Leipzig: 1936; vol. 2, Leipzig: Teubner, 1925. Fascicules have been re-edited by R. Beutler.

Edmonds, J. M., *Elegy and Iambus* (The Loeb Classical Library). Cambridge, Mass.: Harvard University Press, 1954.

———, *Lyra graeca* (The Loeb Classical Library). Cambridge, Mass.: Harvard University Press, 1952–1959.

Evelyn-White, H. G., *Hesiod and the Homeric Hymns* (The Loeb Classical Library). Cambridge, Mass.: Harvard University Press, 1954. For the *Thebais*, see pp. 682–89.

Nauck, A., *Tragicorum Graecorum Fragmenta*, with a supplement by Bruno Snell. Hildesheim: G. Olms, 1964.

BIBLIOGRAPHY

[illegible]